TESTIM

"This is the athletes bible of developing the right habits and mindset. Every young athlete needs to read this book!"

– **Ivan Ljubicic, Coach of Roger Federer & former ATP World nr.3 Ranked Player**

"Once again Allistair has captured the essence of high performance and presented it in an easy to understand, useful form. As a coach, I appreciate both the subtlety and the clarity behind these powerful ideas. A must read for those striving for excellence in any field."

– **Bob Bowman, Longtime Coach of Michael Phelps**

"Allistair is the leading author in leadership, success, and becoming a Champion. In this book, he shares real and important knowledge about the reality of excellence, and I encourage all my athletes and coaches to read his work."

– **Delaney Collins, former Team Canada Ice Hockey Player. Hungarian National Women's Team Coach**

"Allistair is the person I repost the most on social media. His insights are clear & concise yet offer world class guidance for the reader which really resonates with my own philosophy."

**– Nick Matthew OBE,
3 x World Squash Champion & Former World nr.1**

"Allistair has created a one-stop encyclopedia on how to become the best you can be. As an athlete, I read books of a similar theme but never one as rare a read as this; with every turn of the page, each message resonates. Now reading this as a coach, it is a resource I'll be directing all my athletes to."

**– Helen Scott MBE,
5x Paralympic Medalist & World Cycling Champion**

"There is always so much to learn from Allistair. As a former professional player and now coach, I highly recommend this book. It's superb!"

**– Grégory Vignal, Former Liverpool FC &
Glasgow Rangers Player. Dundee FC reserve coach**

HABITS
THAT MAKE A
CHAMPION

First Edition – November 2022

Published by Allistair McCaw

Allistair McCaw

www.AllistairMccaw.com

ISBN: 979-8-218-05399-4

Library of Congress Cataloging-in-Publication Data

Category: Motivation, Mindset, Self-Improvement, Sports

Author: Allistair McCaw

Cover Design & Formatting: Eli Blyden Sr. | www.EliTheBookGuy.com

Printed in the United States of America by Book Bindery: A&A Printing & Publishing | www.PrintShopCentral.com

Disclaimer

Limit of Liability/Disclaimer of Warranty: While the publisher and author have used their best efforts in preparing this book, they make no representations or warranties with respect to the accuracy or completeness of the contents of this book and specifically disclaim any implied warranties of merchantability or fitness for a particular purpose. No warranty may be created or extended by sales representatives or written sales materials. The advice and strategies contained herein may not be suitable for your situation. You should consult with a professional where appropriate. Neither the publisher, the author, the co-writer nor the graphic artist shall be liable for damages.

CONTENTS

HABITS THAT MAKE A CHAMPION

ALLISTAIR McCAW

Introduction

The definition of a 'Champion' can be interpreted differently by every person. A Champion doesn't have to be the most talented individual or the one who stands at the top of the medal podium. A Champion is committed to their vision, excellence, and maximizing everything they've got.

By aiming to become the best version of yourself, you are what I call the '5% Club'. You see, 95% of people out there wish to be great, but they fall short because they aren't willing to do what is required. The fact you are reading this right now tells me you want to be a Champion.

I have worked and consulted with many high achievers and Champions, and I can tell you that the one commonality they all share is this: They all have winning habits.

In this book, you will discover the habits, rituals, and routines of Champions and high performers. You will learn how they think, how they prepare, how they behave, how they compete, and how they deal with their failures and successes. You will also discover that, by mastering your own habits, you gain a powerful strength: Consistency.

No matter how great they become, Champions always remain hungry, humble, and coachable. In this book, my aim is to provide you with the tools, skills, and strategies needed to achieve your goals and realize your greatest potential. I have intentionally made each chapter not longer than a five-minute read to keep the message easy to digest and practical to use.

Finally, there are three questions I always like to ask the athletes and clients I consult or work with, and I pose these questions to you. I believe that before setting out on any goal or dream, it's important to have total clarity on:

1. What is it you want?

2. What do you need to do to achieve it?

3. Why does this mean so much to you?

This book is all about attaining excellence and becoming a creature of Champion habits. It's now time to learn and discover the Habits that make a Champion.

*"First, we build our habits.
Then our habits build us."*

– John Dryden

HABIT 1

THE HABIT OF BEING COACHABLE

"My greatest skill was being teachable. I was like a
sponge. Even if I thought my coaches were wrong,
I tried to listen and learn something."

– Michael Jordan

Before we break down what it means to be coachable, let's start off by saying that being coached is a privilege. You should never take your coaches, or those who help you for granted. It's also good for us to be reminded occasionally that many people around the world will never get the chance or opportunity to play sports, never mind receive coaching.

It doesn't matter how talented you are, if you don't work hard, welcome feedback, and listen to your coaches, you will never reach your maximum potential. Longtime NFL coach of the New England Patriots, Bill Belichick, said, *"It's not about talent. It's about depend-*

ability, consistency, being coachable, and understanding what you need to improve." Being coachable and having a mindset of wanting to continuously learn and improve, are essential to being a Champion.

What does it mean to be coachable? First, as a coachable athlete, you are committed to your own progress and development. You have a greater purpose, or "why," behind your goals. When you are coachable, you put your ego aside and open yourself to listening and learning. No matter how good you become, you are always striving to be better.

Being coachable means you hear feedback, not criticism. Being coachable means you don't take things personally when someone is trying to help you. Being coachable means you look and listen (even if you don't agree with what's being said). Being coachable means being appreciative that someone else cares enough to give you that feedback. As Jesse Kriel, a Rugby World Cup winner from South Africa puts it, *"It's about understanding that the person coaching you wants the best for you."*

If you have a coach that pushes you, challenges you, demands the best from you – then be grateful.

Having such a person in your life is a gift because they probably saw something in you that you maybe didn't see in yourself.

Delaney Collins, a former Canadian National team Ice Hockey player and now a World-class coach in the game, describes a coachable player like this*: "To be a coachable player you need to have humility and never assume you are the perfect or complete athlete. You need to be open to feedback. The athlete may or may not always use that feedback, but they have to take it and try to understand the coach's intention to help them progress as an athlete."*

It is widely known that one of the all-time greats in Basketball, Michael Jordan, was undoubtedly one of the most skilled players to have ever played in the NBA. Of all the skills he had, Michael states that his greatest skill was his coachability. He knew that, by taking in as much knowledge as possible about the sport from every direction, he could use that knowledge when it came to crunch time.

10 Traits of A Coachable Athlete:

1. You take responsibility for your progress
2. You are open-minded and curious
3. You continually want to improve
4. You listen and welcome feedback
5. You have humility
6. You have self-awareness
7. You are respectful of others
8. You are not afraid to try new things
9. You are grateful for the help
10. You are committed to your improvement

Being coachable is both a choice and a skill that can be learned. How you receive and take on feedback as an athlete will ultimately determine how fast or slow your progress will be. Make it your goal to become the most coachable person you know.

How coachable you are comes down to your attitude, not your athleticism.

HABIT 2

THE HABIT OF
DRIVING STANDARDS OF EXCELLENCE

*"Once you say farewell to high standards and
discipline, you say goodbye to success."*

– Sir Alex Ferguson

Whether you are an individual performer or part of a team, your results and outcomes are reflected by your level of commitment and individual standards. Every athlete and team train hard. Every athlete and team want to win. What separates them in the end is to what level of standards and discipline they hold themselves accountable.

Some athletes and teams take responsibility for their actions and behaviors. Unfortunately, others don't. They play dodgeball when it's time to step up and be accountable. They like to make excuses and blame others. They refuse to take responsibility and play the victim instead of the victor.

In all my years, I have never come across a successful person, team, or high performing organization that maintained average standards. Only those who will commit themselves to excellence succeed in the long term. High standards aren't for everyone, but excellence also isn't for everyone.

When describing the *'all-in'* work ethic and high standards of NBA All Star player, Tim Duncan, longtime coach of the San Antonio Spurs, Greg Popovich said, *"In his 19 years playing for the Spurs, Tim was never late to a practice, meal, game, workout, or bus. That's a standard of discipline and reliability that you tend to take for granted."*

Champions hold themselves to a higher standard of excellence and refuse to lower them to accommodate others who refuse to raise theirs. These Champions always aim to set the bar high. Achieving excellence was never meant to be easy and requires a high level of discipline and commitment. This is a big reason many fall short.

There's a great quote from author and professor, Angela Duckworth that goes, *"Gritty people train at the edge of their comfort zone. They zero in on one narrow aspect of their performance and set a stretch goal to improve it."* This is very true. High performing individuals and teams with high standards of excellence are always challenging themselves to be better. Examples of some of those areas include:

- Attitude
- Effort
- Energy
- Work ethic
- Preparation
- Time management
- Communication skills
- Body language

When it comes to standards of excellence in a team environment, the successful teams are made up of members who collaborate well and are open and honest about what is expected of each other. Longtime Duke University Basketball head coach, Mike Krzyzewski, better known as 'Coach K', said, *"In putting together standards, it's essential to involve your whole team.*

Remember, standards are the things that you do all the time and the things for which you hold one another accountable." Some examples of what those standards could be include:

- They always compete hard
- They challenge and push each other to be better
- They put in the extra work without having to be asked
- They communicate and listen well
- They don't tolerate poor behavior or effort

If you maintain a high standard of excellence with the little things, you never have to overthink the big things. I encourage you to take time to establish the standards you will work and live by. In the end, it's your standards that will define you.

You don't need to tell others how invested you are. Your behaviors and actions will show that.

HABIT 3

THE HABIT OF TAKING OWNERSHIP OF YOUR JOURNEY

"Taking complete ownership of your outcomes by holding no one but yourself responsible is the most powerful thing you can do to drive your success."

– Gary W. Keller

Taking ownership isn't always easy, but it's a decision necessary in becoming the best you can be. Taking ownership involves taking responsibility for your choices and decisions. Sometimes you will fall. Mistakes will be made. That's okay. It happens to the best, and it's all part of the learning and growing process.

Casey Stoney, a former England Football captain and someone who has coached top clubs such as Manchester United women's and San Diego Wave FC, describes ownership like this: *"Ownership means that a player takes responsibility for their own learning, behaviors and actions. From my experience, what I have seen is that the players who take ownership are the ones that continue to grow and develop throughout their careers and get to the very top. They are prepared to work hard at their craft and do the things that matter when no one else is watching. They reflect and learn from mistakes and then take action to continue and improve."*

Taking ownership is a fundamental mindset that separates the good from the great athletes. When an individual has a greater sense of self-awareness and takes full ownership of their journey, not only do their game skills improve, but their relationships with their coach and teammates also improve. Ownership is the essence of responsibility or as Casey Stoney likes to put it: *"Ownership is a mentality."*

The legendary Tennessee Basketball coach, Pat Summit, once famously said, *"Responsibility equals accountability, equals ownership, and a sense of ownership is the most powerful weapon a team or organization can have."* Taking ownership of your journey is one of the most impactful choices you can make in life. In my years around top performers, it's a standout trait I've come across when observing Champions. From very early in their careers, these individuals have made the choice to take responsibility for their behaviors and actions. They have adopted a mindset of *'if it's meant to be, it's up to me'.* They understand that the level of success they achieve lies on their shoulders. The author and motivational speaker, Les Brown, once said, *"Accept responsibility for your life. Know that it is you who will get you where you want to go, no one else."*

Champions and high achievers also ensure they have good people around them. This helps them stay on track and make better choices. Unfortunately, we have witnessed athletes make misjudgments, mostly because of poor influences and the environments they find themselves in, especially in the collegiate and professional sports worlds. That's why it's better to hang out with the right people instead of the 'cool' people.

Coaches and athletic recruiters look for athletes who take ownership of their journey. They look for athletes who are responsible, honest, hardworking, and coachable. They look for athletes who are Champion-minded and unafraid to speak up and admit their short-comings or mistakes.

Champion Mentality	Victim Mentality
• Stays positive	• Complains
• Takes responsibility	• Blames others
• Finds solutions	• Makes excuses
• Admits their faults	• Never thinks it's their fault
• Asks for feedback	• Doesn't want feedback

When an athlete takes ownership of their journey, they become accountable for their behaviors and actions. They strive not only to become a better athlete, but also a better person. They recognize that the choices and decisions they make ultimately set them up for either success or failure.

The day you commit to being a Champion is the day you stop accepting 'average'.

HABIT 4

THE HABIT OF
SETTING SMART GOALS

"Set big goals and learn to love the work that gets you to them. Even if you fall short, you'll still be winning."

– Des Linden

Having a vision and setting goals are an essential part of becoming a Champion. Each morning, Champions rise excited about pursuing the goals they have set for themselves. Lebron James, a 4x MVP winner and considered one of the greatest Basketball players of all time said, *"As a professional athlete, a lot will be said about you, but I just try to keep focusing on achieving my goals."* You will discover that great athletes like Lebron, are driven and motivated by the goals they have set for themselves.

Goals provide you with the fuel to do the work. Some advantages of setting goals are that they help increase your direction, motivation, and commitment. They also provide a purpose to what you are doing. The 3 types of goals for every athlete should include:

1. Long-Term Goals:

Long-term goals are what you hope to accomplish in the future. These goals cannot be achieved in a day, a week, or even a month. An example of a long-term goal could be wanting to compete in an event 12 months from now or perhaps the Olympics in four years time.

2. Performance Goals:

These are also known as short-term goals and can be broken into specific categories. Performance goals can be weekly, monthly, or quarterly goals. These help you stay on track and assist with monitoring your progress.

3. Daily Process Goals:

These are the day-to-day goals that work together to help you achieve your performance and longer-term goals. These encompass the daily tasks that connect the performance goals to the outcome goals and include your daily training sessions, sleep habits, nutritional requirements, etc.

For setting goals, Champions adopt the SMART method which is a guide to setting goals and objectives. The SMART method helps push you further, gives you a sense of direction, and helps you organize and reach your goals. SMART goals are:

- **Specific -** knowing what you want to achieve

- **Measurable -** your goal is quantifiable to track progress

- **Attainable -** your goal should challenge you, but still be realistic

- **Relevant -** make sure it is aligned to your purpose

- **Time based -** set a deadline and achievement date

Some things to remember with goal setting is that, as in life, things don't always go according to plan. It is normal to experience unexpected setbacks or interruptions along the way. This could come as an unwanted injury, illness, or personal life happenings. It is important, in these circumstances, to aim to be more open-minded and adaptable when planning your goals.

On a personal note, I always like to share and discuss my goals with at least one other person I know and trust. This keeps me accountable for my targets and ambitions, and receiving much needed encouragement along my journey is helpful, especially on the days when my motivation is low.

A useful tool is to write down your goals and place them somewhere you can see them daily. This is a great motivator and reminder. For example, you could post them on your bedroom or office wall, on the refrigerator, or even on your phone as a wallpaper. Remember, it's only a dream until you write it down.

See it. Believe it. Work for it. Achieve it.

If goals are the fuel that drives our ambition, habits are the engine that helps us get there.

HABIT 5

THE HABIT OF EMBRACING THE WORK

*"Success has to do with deliberate practice.
Practice must be focused, determined,
and in an environment where there's feedback."*
– Malcolm Gladwell

J erry Rice once said, *"Today I will do what others won't, so tomorrow I can accomplish what others can't."* Becoming a mentally tough athlete doesn't just happen overnight. It requires many years of dedicated training and hard work to reach your full potential. It requires grit, resilience, and perseverance. Former World Champion and World record holder for the most consecutive wins, not just in Squash but in all professional sports (555 wins), Jahangir Khan said, *"Without hard work and discipline it is difficult to be a top professional."*

When you embrace the work, progress occurs. When you embrace the work, you build mental toughness. When you embrace the work, excellence happens.

The reality is:
- You won't always feel like it.
- You won't always be motivated.
- You won't always agree with it.
- You won't always want to do it.
- You won't always be excited about it.

But guess what? That's okay. All that matters is that you get up, show up, and never give up. That's what Champions do.

You might think that becoming a Champion involves getting to practice on time and leaving when your coach ends the session – but think again. The others might do that, but you aren't the others. Your goals are different. Becoming a Champion requires a higher level of dedication, commitment, and discipline. It requires doing what others don't want to do.

You're not born mentally tough. You choose to be. It's a skill that is learned and developed. The level of mental toughness you acquire will largely depend on the habits you build and on how disciplined you are in doing the unpleasant and 'hard stuff'. Mental toughness is about embracing difficulty, discomfort and what some like to call *the grind.*

Think, if it was so easy, then everyone would be great at what they do. To master any skill, you are going to have to fall in love with *'the boring'*. In other words, the process of doing the same things over and over. Champions are masters at embracing *'the boring'* as they understand the importance of it. Focused repetition creates the mastery of any skill. As author Daniel Coyle points out, *"There is no substitute for attentive repetition."*

Self-discipline is like a muscle. The more you exercise it, the stronger it gets. One reason why Champions maintain a higher level of focus and drive is because of the commitment to their goals and purpose. When they lose motivation, they tap into the greater reason as to *why* they are doing it. You might remember in the introduction of this book; I posed three questions. The third question was:

Why does this (goal) mean so much to you? This alludes to your deeper motivation and purpose.

Consistency and the ability to handle repetitive work is, without a doubt, one of the main keys to success. It's something NBA Warriors coach, Steve Kerr, credits as a key reason Steph Curry has multiple MVPs to his name. Kerr said, *"It's the consistency of his routine. It's like a metronome. I mean, every day, it's the exact same thing."*

When you are constantly putting in the work and focusing on mastering a skill, it is that consistent effort that will ultimately propel you forward. Remember that progress happens one day at a time. By accumulating the days, one by one, you gradually make progress.

When you're feeling unmotivated or uninspired, think back to why you started in the first place.

HABIT 6

THE HABIT OF
HAVING THE RIGHT BODY LANGUAGE

"Your body language doesn't talk; it screams."

– unknown

Y ou can see a Champion from a mile away. They look like Champions. They act like Champions. You can tell by the way they walk, the way they talk, and the way they present themselves. A Champion shows a humble confidence.

UCONN Women's Basketball coach, Geno Auriemma, is someone who believes that, to become a great player, you need to have great body language. In an interview on the subject, Geno's advice to young players was this: *"Body language matters on the court and on the bench. We put a huge premium on body language, and if your body language is bad, you will never get in the game. Ever. I don't care how good you are."*

Having a positive body language and carrying yourself well are important tools for athletes. Learning how to show confidence through your body language can help you communicate more effectively and earn respect from others. As an athlete, your opponents and teammates can read a lot by observing your body language. They can pick up cues as to how you are feeling. Your body language gives away more than you think.

When it comes to the mind-body relationship, our thoughts dictate how we feel. How we feel dictates how we perform. Poor body language is a decision. Our body language and the way we behave are a result of our thinking. The way we hold our bodies can either raise our energy and confidence or lower it.

Low mental energy leads to low physical energy leads to low performance output.

It's easy to have positive self-talk and good body language when things are going to plan. The real test comes when you face adversity. No one can read your thoughts, but your body language is on display for all to see. As Harvey Wolter said, "*You can tell a lot by someone's body language.*"

Athletes who project poor body language do themselves and their teammates a massive disservice. When an individual displays poor energy and body language in a team setting, it not only disrupts the balance of the team but also indicates a selfish and *'only I matter'* attitude. Their bad energy is contagious and rubs off on those around them.

An athlete with good body language:
- Looks determined and focused
- Keeps their head up and shoulders back
- Radiates a great energy
- Displays a humble confidence
- Walks with purpose

Even if you don't feel confident, practicing positive body language can increase your self-esteem and make you feel better about yourself. Like most other things, improving your body language needs practice. A great way to improve is by making it a priority. To measure your progress, you can score yourself after each practice on a scale of 1-5 on how you did. You can even ask your coaches and teammates to give you feedback on how you're doing.

Your habits will either make or break you. Champions have developed the habit of keeping a positive body language, especially under adversity. There are many uncontrollable factors in sports. However, aiming to keep a good energy and positive body language are things you can maintain power of.

*Your body language is a billboard
for your mental toughness and self-belief.*

HABIT 7

THE HABIT OF
CHOOSING THE RIGHT ENVIRONMENT

"When it comes to your motivation and personal development, it's important as a player to have the right training environment."

– Viktor Axelsen

It's a fact that you become the people you spend the most time with. The more time you spend with the same people, the more you will mirror and reflect their habits, traits, and behaviors – often without even realizing it! In life and in sports, I have always believed that one of the most important decisions you can make is:

Choosing your surroundings in terms of people and environment

41

This will greatly influence the person you become and where you will be in the future. Dr. Benjamin Hardy, an organizational psychologist and a best-selling author, believes that to achieve your goals, you need to ensure you are in the right environment. Our actions and behaviors are a response to the environment we put ourselves in.

As an athlete, having the right coaches and people around you at the right time in your development are key to your progress. You want to constantly be challenging yourself and getting out of your comfort zone. This is what the best performers and Champions do.

Ask any Champion and they will tell you that, as an individual athlete or team player, it's critical to be surrounded by people of great character and competence to succeed. A Champion knows they can't achieve their goals without the guidance, help, and support of a great team around them. If you want to achieve outer success, you need a great inner circle. Althea Gibson, one of the first black athletes to cross the color line of international Tennis and the first African American to win a Grand Slam title once said, *"No matter what accomplishments you make, somebody helped you."*

That's why, as an athlete, it's important to surround yourself with coaches and people of strong character. You need people who challenge you, take you out of your comfort zone and aren't afraid to tell you the truth, especially those who have your best interests at heart and see your full potential. When Alexis Putellas, regarded as one of the world's best female Football players was asked about the importance of having the right environment and people around her who understand her lifestyle and goals, she said, *"I am lucky because my environment knows perfectly what my profession entails and that is why I can enjoy this path."*

10 Traits of a High Performing Training Environment:

1. Involves people of high character
2. Drives high standards and values
3. There is psychological safety
4. Has competent coaches and support personnel
5. Is growth minded

6. There is consistent feedback provided

7. Includes other high performing athletes

8. Provides the appropriate facilities and equipment

9. Motivates the athlete to work harder

10. Teaches life skills, not only athletic skills

Choosing your surroundings in terms of people and environment will greatly influence your future path. If you find that the attitudes, behaviors, and actions of those around you don't align with the goals and aspirations you have for your future, then figure out a way to change your environment. People who drive high standards don't accept or tolerate mediocre surroundings. They don't hang around toxic cultures because they understand how impactful these choices and decisions can affect their future.

What about you? Is your environment pushing you closer to your goals, challenging you to be better, and most of all, making you a better person?

*You are a product of your environment.
Surround yourself with the best.*

H A B I T 8

THE HABIT OF GETTING UP EARLY

"Success comes to those who have the willpower to win over their snooze buttons."

– Unknown

86,400 seconds - that's the time we all get in a day, and how we spend that time ultimately determines our level of success. I've always been in the mindset that our ability to get the best from ourselves comes down to how we manage our energy and time. Your ability to master your life is learning to control where your attention goes. Value what you give your energy and time to.

"If you win the morning, you win the day." Over the years, the high performers and Champions I've come across in my life have all had one thing in common: they all get up early! Getting up early gives you a great advantage over your competition. It gives you a head

start. Studies have suggested that when a person gets up early, they are more energetic, make better choices and are ready to take on challenges. The reason why is that our brain is the most alert in the morning and we think more clearly than at any other time of day. Getting up early also helps us develop the habit of self-discipline.

The Serena Story:

A few years ago, I was working with a professional Tennis player. We had booked a 7:30am practice session at the Stanford University courts whilst at a tournament in California. Upon arrival, we could hear tennis balls being thumped on an outside court. At this time of the morning, when most players would probably still be under the covers sleeping, here was a coach relentlessly feeding ball after ball to a certain female player. Her name? Serena Williams, the 23x Grand Slam Champion. Much the same as Kobe Bryant, who liked to get his 400 practice shots in before breakfast, Serena had been on the court for over an hour. While the rest are tucked into their beds dreaming about success, the Champions are already out there working hard, drenched in sweat. Like the Serena's and Kobe's, Champions are built far away from the crowds, cameras, and noise. They are built when no one is around.

Personally, as an athlete, I always loved being up early and working hard, knowing that probably 95% of my competitors were still asleep. It gave me confidence. I would say that I credit most of my athletic success to the training sessions I did on those early mornings when it was still dark outside. A lot of my grit and discipline were built during those lonely, early morning sessions.

5 Benefits to Getting Up Early:

1.   There are fewer distractions
2.   It gives you more time in your day
3.   Helps you prepare for the day ahead
4.   Gives you more time to have a good breakfast
5.   In warmer climates, you can beat the heat

Studies have proven that, if you get into the routine of '*early to bed and early to rise*', you are more likely to have a better sleeping pattern, which leads to being more energetic and productive throughout the day. When this happens, you can accomplish your routines and goals much easier.

Getting up early helps you win the day. When you develop this habit, you'll reap the benefits of the many good routines that lead to success. Like the Champions, aim to get into the habit of beating the alarm clock. While the rest are dreaming about success, you are already out there working for it!

Champions are built far away from the crowds, cameras, and noise.
They are built when no one is around.

HABIT 9

THE HABIT OF POSITIVE SELF TALK

*"Be mindful of your self-talk.
It's a conversation with the universe."*

– David James

The mind is everything. What you think is what you become. Champions have developed an internal dialogue that empowers them. They have worked to develop this habit over many years of practice. They are aware that their body hears everything their mind is thinking and saying.

Perhaps you don't realize it, but we subconsciously talk to ourselves all the time. According to psychology experts at Queen's University in Canada, the average person will typically have over 6,000 thoughts in a single day! Our minds are constantly communicating to us.

Our inner voice and self-talk can become either our greatest friend or fiercest enemy. Tony Dungy, a former

American Football coach and now sports analyst said, *"Be positive. Your mind is more powerful than you think. What is down in the well comes up in the bucket. Fill yourself with positive things."* How we talk to ourselves can greatly affect how we behave, feel, and perform. A person who says to herself *'I can't'* has already lost half the battle. Everyone has an inner voice that either encourages or criticizes, and it's our thoughts that strongly influence our performances and how we feel. Champions know that the way they talk to themselves massively influences their outcomes.

We can talk ourselves into or out of almost anything. A great quote that emphasizes how attitude and mindset determine our success or failure comes from Henry Ford. He said, *"Whether you think you can, or you think you can't – you're right."* It's a known fact that we can mindfully steer our inner dialogue by consciously thinking productive and empowering thoughts, especially under adverse or difficult situations.

Positive thinking won't always guarantee that you win, but negative thinking will almost always guarantee that you don't. Your biggest competition isn't your opponent. Your biggest competition is YOU. Every single day you are competing against the voice in your head and the belief in your heart.

Just think about it; during competition, when do we most need empowering self-talk, positive body language, and a winning attitude? Answer: When things aren't going so well. However, instead, what often happens is we get negative and become our own worst enemies. As a result, our energy and confidence evaporate. Don't let this happen to you!

As an athlete, it's so important to be mindful of how you talk to yourself. We build our self-image and confidence by thinking more positively about ourselves. What is real confidence, you ask? Real confidence is about self-acceptance. It's when you don't feel the need to prove or compare yourself to anyone else. Real confidence is about self-belief and talking to yourself in an uplifting and empowering way.

Like any other learned skill, developing confidence and better self-talk requires practice and takes time. Initially, you might find it difficult, but the more you practice self-talk, the more your confidence will soar.

Know there is incredible power in your self-talk. The words you say to yourself can either propel you forwards or hold you back. You can become your own greatest supporter or your own biggest enemy. The choice is yours.

Self-talk is the most powerful form of communication there is. It can either empower you or defeat you.

HABIT 10

THE HABIT OF CELEBRATING THE 'SMALL WINS'

"The great victory, which appears so simple today, was a result of a series of small victories that went unnoticed."

– Paulo Coelho

Not all victories need to be large to make an impact. The 'small wins' that are made daily eventually lead to the bigger wins in the long term. The key to success, whether it be in sport, business, or life is to focus on all those little victories and 'small wins'. Let me explain further...

As someone striving for progress and excellence, it's natural to only notice the mistakes and failures we make. We can so easily beat ourselves up over a poor performance and become our own worst enemy. The problem with this is that we end up self-sabotaging and denying ourselves of success. On top of this, we also take the joy out of what we do.

The 'small wins' we make are often the things we can so easily overlook or take for granted. The 'small wins' are subtle. They don't jump out at you. For example, it could be arriving early to practice and getting in a good warm up, completing a tough practice when you weren't feeling 100%, or achieving a personal best in pull ups at the gym. **By taking the time to recognize and celebrate the 'small wins', you not only grow your wall of confidence but also increase your motivation, enjoyment, and desire to work even harder.**

Even when everything isn't going perfect, Champions develop the habit of focusing on the positives and 'small wins' instead of being weighed down by the negatives. In fact, I've witnessed athletes who weren't 100% prepared game-wise but succeeded because they showed up with the right mindset. They showed up with a Champion's attitude.

There is incredible power in developing the habit of celebrating the 'small wins'. Recognizing them helps us track all the incremental and sometimes unseen steps involved in achieving our longer-term goals. Kara Goucher, one of America's best long-distance runners said, *"Acknowledge all of your small victories. They will eventually add up to something great."*

We can so easily overlook the small victories because we are too busy looking for the big stuff. We should still be excited and proud of ourselves when we achieve something big, but there are many more opportunities to celebrate the smaller wins.

Got extra reps in before practice? – Celebrate it!
Kept a cool head when under pressure? – Celebrate it!
Achieved a personal best at practice? – Celebrate it!
Received a good score on your exam? – Celebrate it!
Achieved all your mini goals for today? – Celebrate it!

In developing Champion-like habits, it's crucial to acknowledge and reflect on your 'small wins'. Those mini doses of encouragement will fuel your mental strength to keep you motivated and enjoying what you are doing, especially during the more challenging times.

Celebrating your 'small wins' can give you the boost you need to keep going. It is also important to remember that It's hard to burn out when you find joy and meaning in what you do. When you love what you do, you want to do more of it. When you do more of it, you become better at it.

Success can be a series of small victories. Celebrate every win, no matter how small. Learn to give yourself the same appreciation you would so naturally give others. The 'small wins' build progress. The 'small wins' build motivation. The 'small wins' build momentum. The 'small wins' build confidence.

Celebrate any progress, no matter how small. Don't wait to get perfect. Recognizing your efforts each day helps build your confidence and motivation.

HABIT 11

THE HABIT OF GOOD TIME MANAGEMENT

"I was taught a strong work ethic which included punctuality, which I've always felt is a sign of respect for others."

– Nicole Kidman

I t was during a break at a conference I was speaking at in Los Angeles where I was conversing with the CEO of a sports management company based there. In our conversation, I was intrigued to ask him what his approach was for hiring new employees. Besides the obvious attributes such as good organizational and interpersonal skills, the one thing that caught my attention was 'punctuality'.

He mentioned that when hiring someone new for the company, they always noted what time the prospect arrived for their interview and how well they had prepared for it. He said that if the prospect was late or even on time for the meeting, that would already be a red flag.

Now, you may think what has this got to do with being an athlete or high performer? The answer is a lot! When striving for excellence, you are all about the small details, especially with time management. High performers are time sticklers. Former head coach of the England women's Football team, Hope Powell said, *"There are a lot of positives to come out of playing sport, not just Football. Sport improves your time management. You have to be at places on time and disciplined in terms of training."*

Legendary NFL Football coach, Vince Lombardi, was also known for punctuality. He drove high standards and discipline, which is, no doubt, one of the many reasons he won five Super Bowls as a head coach. One of his standards was that he expected his players and assistant coaches to be at least 15 minutes early to meetings and practices. Not on time, but 15 minutes early. If they weren't, he considered them late. This came to be known as *'Lombardi time'.*

The advantage of having good time management is that it sets you up for success. Arriving at a meeting or practice *before time* instead of *on time* allows you to be more relaxed and prepared. The opportunity to set up your equipment, warm up, and even get some extra reps in occurs by arriving early. It also sends a strong message to your teammates and coaches on your level of commitment. It promotes that you are serious about improving and getting the best out of yourself and those around you. It also sends a signal about what kind of culture you aspire to create.

Daily productivity comes from effective time management. This starts from the moment you wake until the time you rest your head on the pillow at night. We all get the same number of hours in a day, and how we use that time determines our level of success or failure. Champions and high performers manage their time well.

5 Reasons it Pays to Keep Good Time Management:

1. You'll arrive better prepared and ready

2. It shows you respect the time of others

3. You'll show others you are a reliable person

4. You'll be less stressed

5. You'll be able to do extra reps

Like Champions, develop the habit of great time management. Champions arrive early and are prepared. The time you arrive tells a lot about your character and the standards you keep.

"If you are 5 minutes early,
you are already 10 minutes late."

– Vince Lombardi

HABIT 12

THE HABIT OF CONSISTENCY

"Success isn't always about greatness. It's about consistency. Consistent hard work leads to success. Greatness will come."

– Dwayne Johnson

Richard G. Scott once said, *"We become what we want to be by consistently being what we want to become each day."* After being involved in elite sports for well over three decades now, I've learned that discipline and consistency are what separate the good from the great performers.

What you will discover is that the average athletes will do what is needed only sometimes. The good athletes will do what is needed most of the time. But the great athletes will do what is needed all the time. Consistency is what transforms average into excellence.

Ask any Champion and they will tell you that you cannot become great at something without having a high level of discipline and consistency. A Champion knows that, especially on the days when you aren't feeling up for it, those matter the most. A Champion gets it done.

When a Champion is asked to put in the extra reps
— they do it.

When a Champion is asked to work on their mindset
— they do it.

When a Champion is asked to get uncomfortable
— they do it.

Champions do what needs to be done whether they feel like it or not.

Building consistency into your life is one key to success. The Greek philosopher, Aristotle once said, *"We are what we repeatedly do. Excellence is not an act, but a habit."* When I hear this quote, I immediately think of the most decorated Olympian of all time, Michael Phelps. The American swimmer admits that one key to having had such a successful career came down to his discipline and consistency in doing what needed to be done, even on the days when he didn't feel like it. His commitment to excellence and the habits he had built over the years paved his road to success.

Positive Small Habits & Choices + Consistency + Time = Excellence

A few years back, when I was consulting at Duke University, I had the privilege of spending some time with the legendary Basketball coach, Mike Krzyzewski. While talking to 'Coach K' in his office one afternoon, I asked him what standout qualities he had seen in the best athletes during his 45+ years as a coach. Without hesitation he said, *"The best athletes are the consistent ones. They have created habits of excellence in their life. That's what makes them Champions."*

It's not only consistency in your preparation that makes you a Champion, but also consistency in your mindset. Champions have built the habit and skill set of controlling their emotions to perform well.

Roger Federer, the 20x Grand Slam Tennis Champion, will admit that he was not always the cool, calm, and collected athlete we all admired over the years. During his younger years, Roger had to work on controlling his emotions and anger. Through hard work and discipline, he developed consistent habits that led to him becoming arguably one of the greatest Tennis players of all time.

Remember, to become a Champion, it's not what you do sometimes that matters, it's what you do all of the time. Aim to become more disciplined in your daily habits and behaviors. Consistency is what separates the best from the rest.

Champions are Champions not because they do anything extraordinary, but because they do the ordinary things consistently well.

H A B I T   1 3

THE HABIT OF
GETTING UNCOMFORTABLE

"The one thing you learn is when you can step out of your comfort zone and be uncomfortable, you see what you're made of and who you are."

– Sue Bird

They say that 'a *comfort zone is a no-progress zone'*, and in my experience of being around high performers and Champion athletes, there could be nothing more accurate than that statement. Once you get comfortable, you get complacent.

Wikipedia describes a *comfort zone* as, *"… a psychological state in which things feel familiar to a person and they are at ease and (perceive they are) in control of their environment, experiencing low levels of anxiety and stress. In this zone, a steady level of performance is possible".*

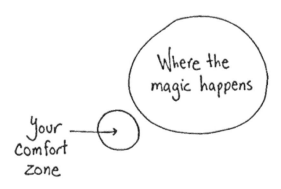

Anyone who achieved greatness, has pushed far and beyond their limits and comfort zone. These individuals have done the things others don't want to do or feel like doing. They have challenged and pressed themselves time and time again. As they like to say, *'if it doesn't challenge you, it doesn't change you'.*

When pursuing excellence or a challenging long-term goal, understand that not everyone will agree or go along with your journey. That's okay because it's your goal, not theirs, and those who seek excellence are on a different path. Champions embrace discomfort. They don't take shortcuts or make excuses. They stay disciplined and do the hard stuff, even on the days they don't feel like it. Let's face it, everyone can do it when they feel like it. It's on the days when it is just that little more difficult - that's what makes the difference.

95% of people live in a comfort zone. When things get tough, they default to taking the easier way out. They develop a belief they can't do it. They make excuses and develop unhelpful habits that don't push them forwards. The truth is that nine out of ten times, it's your mind, not your body, that holds you back. By developing the right habits and mindset, you can get rid the self-doubt and overcome almost any obstacle or challenge. Remember: **You always win in the mind first.**

All growth starts at the end of your comfort zone. To move to a new level in your life, you must break through your comfort zone and do the things that are uncomfortable. I've always been of the belief that too much comfort makes you complacent while too much luxury makes you lazy. It's something I subscribe to, as our growth will always be contingent on our willingness to be uncomfortable.

Bad habits are like a comfortable bed: easy to get into but hard to get out of. Being in a comfort zone can become a habit that takes you further away from what you want to achieve. It leads to complacency, and Champions don't allow themselves to get complacent.

Push yourself. Embrace the uncomfortable. Because nobody else is going to do it for you.

HABIT 14

THE HABIT OF BEING PRESENT

*"I kept telling myself this word, process.
Focus on my process, don't care about the result."*

– Rory McIlroy

One of the most powerful weapons a Champion possesses is their ability to eliminate distraction and be focused and present in the moment. When asked what Basketball legend Michael Jordan's key attributes were to being such a great player, Phil Jackson, his former coach at the Chicago Bulls, said, *"Michael's gift was not that he could jump high, run fast, or shoot a basketball. His gift was that he was present. And that was a separator."*

I'm sure you will agree that, when practicing or competing, it's so easy to be distracted by external things. Our thoughts can often be exacerbated when nervous, anxious, or when feeling pressure. The feeling of sweaty palms, elevated heart rate, or erratic breathing can take over our emotional state and throw us completely off-track. This can result in either *'freezing up'* or *'choking',* which is defined as a sub-optimal sporting performance delivered when under pressure. This occurs when, initially, we are firmly in command of our performance, but then, our mental state changes which affects the outcome. Such thoughts as, "*I hope I don't mess it up like last time*" or, "*if I make this play, then I am one point away from the Championship'',* enter the mind and you are no longer in the present moment. If you have ever experienced this, I have some good news for you - it even happens to the world's very best performers. So, take heart, you are not alone!

Ok, but how do I fix this you ask? Well, one way I like to help my athletes is with the technique I call P.O.P (Power of Presence):

Stage 1: Early recognition

Early awareness is needed to avoid overthinking or choking. You may feel such things as a tightness in the chest or nerves kicking in. We should aim to catch these before they catch us. Our past experiences will usually help with this.

Stage 2: Slowing down breathing and heart rate

Focus on slowing down your breathing by taking relaxed deep breaths to help decrease the heart rate. This will help with calming the nerves and enable you to regain composure.

Stage 3: Use positive mantras to regain focus

The third stage uses positive self-talk through mantras. For example, you could say to yourself, *"I'm calm and in control"* or *"right here, right now".* By doing this, you are consciously bringing yourself back to the present moment.

Maria Sharapova was one of the most focused athletes to have played Tennis. If you ever got to watch her play live or see her on video, you would notice the five-time Grand Slam Champion continually talking to herself and encouraging herself between points. She had a habit and ritual of tapping her thigh before receiving a serve from her opponent. This was a way for her to stay focused and present. Maria was also one of the best players to stay calm under pressure.

Champions thrive under pressure. They stay positive and calm. They view pressure as an opportunity to do something great. I encourage you to try the P.O.P technique next time you feel nervous, lose focus, or get a little anxious. As with your game skills, being present and staying in the moment takes time to develop. It takes practice and patience is key!

Be so engaged in the process that you even forget the score.

HABIT 15

THE HABIT OF SELF-BELIEF

"Your belief determines your action, and your action determines your result, but first you have to believe."
– Mark Victor Hansen

Great things stem from great self-belief. Champions know that having confidence and an unshakable self-belief in themselves is vital for success. Something I like to remind the athletes I work with is this: You can be the hardest working athlete, but without belief in your work, your chances of success will always be limited.

Hard Work + Belief In The Work = Success

The 2019 Champions League Football semi-final between Barcelona FC and Liverpool FC is a great case study when it comes to belief. Barcelona, who boasted players such as Lionel Messi and Luis Suarez, were leading 3-0 going into their second leg match at Anfield. For Liverpool to come back from this deficit was deemed almost impossible by the pundits, especially as they were missing two of their star players, Mo Salah and Roberto Firmino. In one of the most memorable comebacks in the competition's history, Liverpool eventually won 4-3. When their coach, Jurgen Klopp, was asked what made the difference, he said, *"My players brought the right attitude. Despite the odds against us winning, they never stopped believing."*

Champions believe they can achieve anything they set their mind to. Ask professional Swimmer Kyle Chalmers, a world record holder and Olympic gold medalist. In an interview with the Australian Champion, he said, *"If I'm in the right mindset, I believe I can win anything, any distance, any day. Probably not realistic, but that's just my mindset."*

However, elite athletes like Kyle aren't delusional into thinking they can achieve great things without being 100% committed and putting in the hard work. They know there is no elevator to success. You must take the stairs.

The truth about confidence and self-belief is that no one is just born with it. You are not born a winner. You are not born a loser. You are born a chooser. Fortunately, our mindset, our emotions, and our behavior are under our influence. Developing a mindset of belief takes work and the things we say to ourselves play a massive role in this. We become what we think.

Throughout your athletic journey, you will go through periods of indecision and self-doubt. That's normal. At times, we can often find ourselves in certain situations and circumstances that can negatively affect our confidence and self-esteem, e.g., a slump in form or a poor run of performances and results. Every athlete will go through periods of difficulty and uncertainty, but how we reclaim that lost confidence or self-belief is key.

One way you can rebuild lost confidence and belief is by what I term, *'taking a history lesson'.* Sometimes it's helpful to look back at your best athletic performances and highlights. You might even have videos of yourself you can watch. This is a great way to remind yourself that you have done it before, and you can do it again. By *taking a history lesson*, it can help reignite, motivate, and inspire you.

Another way to build your self-belief and confidence is through mantras. By continually repeating a chosen word or phrase to yourself, you eventually believe it. Again, we become what we think and say to ourselves.

Aimee Mullins, a former world record holder and Paralympian in Track and Field once said, *"Belief in oneself is infectious. It generates momentum, the collective force of which far outweighs any kernel of self-doubt that may creep in."*

You get to choose your mindset. A few ways you can build your self-belief are:

- Focusing more on your strengths
- Recognizing your daily effort and progress
- Setting realistic and achievable goals
- Aiming for excellence, not perfection
- Surrounding yourself with supportive people
- Finding joy and having fun in what you do
- Looking back at your past successes

*Great things stem from a great
self-belief. To achieve it,
you must first believe it.*

H A B I T 1 6

THE HABIT OF
CONTROLLING THE CONTROLLABLES

*"You may not control every situation and its outcome,
but you can control your attitude and
how you deal with it."*

– unknown

"When you can't control what's happening, challenge yourself to control how you respond. That's where your power is." Champions understand that worrying or giving attention to things that aren't within their control is a waste of energy. Instead, they focus on things they can control.

Most sports involve a physical, tactical, technical, and mental component. As an athlete, you have a limited amount of physical and emotional energy, so by wasting time on the things you have no control over, you will only empty your energy tank and lead yourself to frustration and a decrease in performance. However, when you focus more of your attention on the things you can control, it gives you a direct influence on your destiny and outcomes.

It's a fact that every athlete must face mentally challenging situations throughout their playing career, many being out of their control. However, it is how the athlete approaches and overcomes these obstacles that determines how far they progress. As motivational speaker, Wayne Dyer said, *"I cannot always control what goes on outside. But I can always control what goes on inside."*

Controllables	Uncontrollables
Behavior	Weather
Attitude	Playing surface
Focus	Umpire
Emotions	Unruly spectators
Body language	Bad luck
Self-talk	Last minute changes

Your coach determines the number of minutes you get to play in a team sport. If you are on the bench, your attitude and energy will often determine how long you stay there. Complaining or sulking will only reinforce your coach's opinion of you as a player. This kind of behavior isn't only being selfish but will also garner you less playing time, not more. Something to also note here is that the attitudes on a bench reveal a lot about a team's togetherness and culture.

'Can Do' vs 'Can't Do' attitude:

We all know that injuries can be a setback, but you are still in control of your attitude and how you respond to it. Instead of bemoaning your ill fortune or 'bad luck', you could wisely use that free time to work on other areas in your game. Reviewing videos, scouting opponents, or working on developing your mental skills are all valuable activities whilst in rehabilitation. You could even do strengthening exercises that don't directly impact the recovery of your injury. **It's about focusing on having a 'can do' attitude instead of a 'can't do' one.**

Focusing on the things you can't control, worrying about what the future may bring, and complaining about your current situation are what make up a loser's mindset. Instead of wasting time and energy on what's not in your control, do what the great ones do - adopt the mindset of a Champion and focus on what you can control. Controlling the controllables positively affects your destiny, and your performance is not dictated by outside forces. Isn't that what you want?

Champions train.
Losers complain.

HABIT 17

THE HABIT OF "WINNING THE DAY"

"Your future is created by what you do today, not tomorrow."

– Robert Kiyosaki

Everyone wants to win, but how many are willing to do what it takes? How many are willing to go the extra mile? How many are willing to get uncomfortable? These are the burning questions. As Sue Bird, the WNBA Basketball player said, *"The one thing you learn is when you can step out of your comfort zone and be uncomfortable, you see what you're made of and who you are".*

"*Daily wins lead to a lifetime of success.*" It's been said that the key to success is developing '*the will to win,*' but this is not worth anything without having the commitment and discipline to do what it takes to prepare to win.

Champions wake up each day aiming to '*win the day*'. I first heard this phrase when reading up on the former Oregon Ducks Football Head Coach, Chip Kelly. I was always intrigued by Kelly's coaching style and his ability to change the culture of a program by incorporating this mantra. He believed that, to win the end of season Championship, you had to first win *today.*

This meant winning every practice session, wind sprint, gym session, scrimmage, meeting, and then, the game. To Kelly, absolutely everything mattered, and every detail was accounted for. Winning the day was about having the right mindset and being focused on the task at hand. It was about accomplishing all the small daily goals and not looking too far ahead.

When I asked Paul Coll, New Zealand's first ever number one ranked Squash player in the world, what it meant to him to '*win the day', he said*, "*I win the day by first winning the morning. I have a morning routine. Outside of competition, I wake up at the same time and start with 2-3 minutes of slow nasal breathing, followed by 1-2 rounds of Hof breathing, and then a 3-minute cold shower. This helps me start my day with more energy and a positive outlook."*

Much the same as in Paul's case, when you begin to closely look at the daily routines and habits of Champions, you quickly learn that their success isn't only about what they do on the court or in the playing arena, but what they do the days away from it. They *'win the day'* by accomplishing what needs to be done today.

10 Examples of How You Can 'WIN THE DAY':

1. Plan your day the night before

2. Have a set time to wake up

3. Make your bed – it's your first win of the day

4. Hydrate - constantly sip water throughout the day

5. Arrive at least 20-30 minutes before practice to prepare

6. Bring a winner's attitude and mindset

7. Aim to win the warmup, the practice, the cool down, etc

8. Ask your coaches for feedback after the practice

9. Perform all your post-recovery routines after practice

10. Spend some time journaling

Adopt the attitude and habit to do every task, regardless of its nature, to the best of your ability. When you consistently take care of all the small things daily, that's when excellence occurs. **Excellence is in the details**. Be invested, because when you love the process, you'll love what the process does for you.

How do you *'WIN THE DAY'*?

Daily wins and habits are the compound interests of future success.

HABIT 18

THE HABIT OF
PRACTICING UNDER PRESSURE

"The only thing that relieves pressure is preparation."

— Tom Kite

L et me start by asking you this question: In sports, how do you view pressure? Do you view it as a threat and something you'd rather avoid at all costs? Or do you view pressure as an exciting challenge, something that gets your adrenaline pumping? When I ask Champions this question, they choose the latter every time.

Dealing with pressure comes down to three things:

1. How you view it

2. How you prepare for it

3. How you deal with it

How you perceive pressure is critical to your performance and outcomes. Greg Louganis, a five-time Olympic medalist and the first man in Olympic history to sweep the Diving events in consecutive Olympic Games, was asked how he dealt with pressure in competition. He answered it with this: *"When you walk into that arena, there's an energy, it is palpable. If you interpret that energy as pressure, you're more apt to implode. But if you interpret that pressure as energy and inspiration, it can catapult you to levels you never dreamed possible."* Greg chose to view pressure as a positive energy. Additionally, he prepared for it during practice by using methods such as visualization and breathing techniques.

Another great example of dealing with pressure in a different form comes from the most decorated Olympian athlete of all times, Michael Phelps. During a practice session, his longtime coach, Bob Bowman, purposely stood on Michael's goggles resulting in Michael having to swim the whole session with broken goggles and water in his eyes. Fast forward to the 2008 Olympics in Beijing; it was in the 200-meter butterfly event where Phelps was going for his 10th gold medal of his career when disaster struck. Upon diving into the pool, Michael's goggles broke, and he could hardly see anything. However, the fortunate thing was that he had prepared for this 'surprise' moment and claimed yet another gold medal and world record.

Under pressure, you will revert to your level of preparation and habits. Poor habits will result in poor outcomes. Good habits will result in more favorable ones. That's why it's important to train and instill helpful habits and techniques so they're ingrained into your muscle memory. To perform well under pressure, your self-talk and self-belief must be stronger than your fears and doubts.

The one thing you'll discover in all the best athletes is that they handle the pressure moments better. The two main reasons behind this comes down to how they view pressure (mindset) and how they practice (preparation). The best athletes choose to see pressure as a positive. In competition, when the pressure moments arrive, they have already put themselves in those 'moments' and situations. During practice, they have gone to battle. As American Basketball coach, Tom Crean, once said,

"During practice, average players get bored, good players get better, great players go to battle."

Not only are the best athletes technically, tactically, and physically ready, but they are also mentally ready to handle moments of pressure. Their training is designed around the level of pressure they will face in competition. They don't have 'soft' practices. That's why, when it comes to competition time, Champions thrive when pressure arrives. Michael Jordan said, *"I played hard every day in practice; so playing hard in a game was just a habit."*

Champions view pressure as:

- An opportunity to put their skills to the test
- A positive energy and adrenaline
- A great challenge
- An opportunity to learn and improve

If you don't practice under pressure, then how do you expect to get it right come competition time?

HABIT 19

THE HABIT OF JOURNALING

"Writing down your feelings in a journal or notebook can help clear out negative thoughts and emotions that keep you feeling stuck."

– Serena Williams

Champion athletes are constantly looking for any edge they can get. They are systematically training to improve all the technical, tactical, physical, and mental factors associated with their sport. The most effective way for an athlete to monitor their progress is through a training journal or app. By incorporating this daily activity, self-reflection and improvement are tracked.

Some of the world's greatest minds from history have been known to journal such as Marcus Aurelius, Maya Angelou, Michelle Obama, Charles Darwin, Winston Churchill, and Isaac Newton. Even 4x Formula 1 World Champion, Sebastian Vettel, was famous for keeping a notebook and journaling his thoughts on how his car performed and how he felt at the end of team testing days or qualifying sessions. He also kept notes of every race track he competed on around the world.

Organization and planning are undoubtedly two of the biggest keys to training effectively. A successful athlete is a well-organized athlete. Starting a training log or journal is one of the best ways to systemize and keep track of your training. It's also a great way for athletes to immerse themselves in the journey.

As a former professional athlete, a habit I integrated into all my training sessions and daily activities for more than 20 years was journaling. I remember with pride, sitting down at the end of each day to record things such as my morning resting heart rate, sleep and all the training specifics I'd completed that day. By performing this daily ritual, I recorded all my training and kept track of how my body was responding to the workload and sleep patterns, nutrition, and recovery. I also reviewed which training methods were working or not. By consistently journaling over all those years, I built an archive of information that would help me understand if I was progressing or regressing. Journaling was always something that helped keep me focused and stay motivated.

Journaling after competing is also a valuable tool for athletes. Tracking such things as who your opponent was that day, the result, how you performed, what strategies you adopted, what worked, what didn't, etc. will help you for future reference and ongoing development.

Journaling is a personal and very individual process. What you choose to track is entirely up to you. It could even include things such as your thoughts and feelings.

TIP: A great way to improve your mindset is to record your 'Controllables' after each practice and match. Here the athlete scores themselves between one and five (one being poor and five being excellent). Such controllables and behaviors to score could include your:

- Rituals and routines

- Focus

- Attitude

- Body language

- Self-talk

Perhaps the greatest advantage of journaling is that it increases your confidence, improves your self-discipline, and increases memory retention. By getting into the habit of journaling each day, you will also gain more self-awareness.

Champions track their progress by journaling daily. It's a habit that helps them self-reflect and improve.

HABIT 20

THE HABIT OF
NOT TAKING SHORTCUTS

"If you do the work, you get rewarded. There is no shortcut to success."

– Michael Jordan

A lifelong lesson I learned at a young age was from a high school coach I had back in South Africa. She said, *"Champions don't take shortcuts."* This simple message has stuck with me to this day.

During my lifetime, I've never met a true Champion who cut corners, took shortcuts, or stopped short of the lines. Maybe the reason is because a Champion understands there are no shortcuts to any places worth going.

It's been said that the true test of a man's character is what he does when no one is watching. Being honest and truthful with ourselves is not always easy, but it is important if we are to maximize our abilities in sport and in life. People with good character and work ethic are less likely to look for shortcuts. Even when their coach is not around or they are left to practice alone, **Champions maintain a standard of excellence.** They take ownership and practice with the same intensity and focus. Laura Wilkinson, an Olympic gold medalist in Diving, said, *"A Champion is defined when no one is watching or cheering you on. Traits such as perseverance, resilience, grit, and self-control are developed when the athlete takes ownership."*

Ask any Champion who has achieved excellence; they will tell you that there are no easy routes or shortcuts to success. If you are constantly looking for the shortcuts, you aren't only going to fall short of doing the work required to become your best, but you also limit your ability to build a Champion mentality. When I asked Mickey Arthur, a World-class International Cricket coach what he'd seen in the best players he'd worked with, he said, *"Champions are self-driven to be the best and determined to follow great routines – technically, mentally, physically, and tactically. Taking shortcuts simply doesn't pay off if you want to be a great cricketer."*

There's a great quote by the English writer and poet, J.R.R Tolkien that goes, *'Shortcuts make long delays.'* Nothing could be closer to the truth with sport because, when you make it easier for yourself, you eventually pay the price in competition. The habits you've created during practice time become your default come game day. Michael Jordan once said, *"There are no shortcuts. I approached practices the same way I approached games. You can't turn it on and off like a faucet. I couldn't dog it during practice and then, when I needed that extra push late in the game, expect it to be there. Very few people get anywhere by taking shortcuts."*

Champions don't skip reps or do things half-heartedly. They understand that, when you stop short of the line or cut corners, you aren't only tricking your coach and your teammates, you're tricking yourself. Champions stay accountable and know that every little choice, decision, and step of their journey contributes to their overall success.

A Champion does the hard work even when their coach isn't around or watching. A Champion is someone who doesn't need to be asked to do the extra work. A

Champion is someone who doesn't make excuses or blame others when things go wrong. A Champion will raise the standard and do more than what's been asked of them. A Champion has developed the habit of doing the hard stuff, even when they don't feel like undertaking it.

There's a reason only a select few do great things in sports and in life. Success leaves clues and lazy people don't make it. Observe the Champions and best teams, and you'll see they don't cut lines or take shortcuts. They drive standards of excellence every single day. They choose the right way over the easy way every time.

Champions don't cut corners or take shortcuts. It's a standard they hold for themselves.

HABIT 21

THE HABIT OF TAKING ACTION

"You can sit here and dream about it or you can go out and make it happen."

– Unknown

Champions don't sit around and wait for things to happen. They know that, if they want something, it's on them to go out and get it. Champions are well prepared and take consistent daily action. What sets them apart is that they've already put in the work long before the opportunity arrives. They believe that, when you stay ready, you don't need to get ready. It's a lesson in business and in life too. Richard Whitehead, a Paralympian gold medalist and World record holder said, *"Life need not have limits. Having an opportunity in life is important, but what defines you is what you do with that opportunity."*

Preparation + Opportunity + Action = Achievement

Champions stay accountable and wake up with a daily plan. They know that, if they want to achieve their goals, it's up to them to do the work. These individuals are opportunists and understand that to become successful involves taking risks. Ann Meyers, a trailblazer in women's Basketball said, *"If somebody gives you an opportunity, say yes to it. So, what if you fail? You won't know if you fail or succeed unless you try."*

Did you know that one of the most important keys to success comes down to planning and commitment? While the thinkers are still thinking, the doers are already hard at work. As author and leadership expert, Tony Robbins, said, *"The one thing that separates winners from the losers is that winners take action."*

When Champions are struggling or facing challenges, they don't bemoan their bad luck and say, *"Why me?"* They respond. They devise a plan and get back on the horse. Educator and motivational speaker, Nick Vujicic, said, *"To wish for change will change nothing. To make the decision to take action right now will change everything."*

Champions change before they must. They know that, if they are lacking in a particular area of their game, be it mentally, physically, technically, or tactically, they will seek the guidance of an expert, coach, or mentor. As an athlete, it's important that you know what you need to do, and who you need, to make it to the next level. You might remember in the introduction at the beginning of this book, I asked you three questions. The second of those three questions were: **What do you need to do to achieve it?** This is an action step. Remember that, at certain times in your development and career, you will need different voices and opinions to help further your progress.

A lesson I've learned when it comes to getting things done is that you need to push yourself because nobody else will do it for you. How many people do you know that talk about their goals and plans all the time but nothing ever seems to happen?

How many times have you heard someone say:

- I want to start a podcast – but never do?
- I want to run a marathon – but never do?
- I want to start a new career – but never do?
- I want to improve my fitness – but never do?
- I want to learn another language – but never do?

Champions take measures and keep making the steps daily. Some days there will be big steps made, some days they will be smaller ones. But all that matters is that they keep making the steps. They stay disciplined and commit to the plan. The difference lies in taking daily consistent action. As Pablo Picasso once said, *"Action is the foundational key to all success."*

Champions know that success lies on the other side of your comfort zone.

HABIT 22

THE HABIT OF BRINGING THE RIGHT ATTITUDE

"A bad attitude is like a flat tire. If you don't change it, you'll never go anywhere."

– Unknown

Nick Bollettieri is regarded as one of the most famous names in Tennis. For a couple of years, I had the opportunity and privilege to learn and be mentored by him whilst at his academy in Bradenton, Florida. Something Nick always liked to remind me of was that one of the most important choices we can make in sports, and in life, is the attitude we choose. Nick's positivity and energy would always rub off on you. The master coach believed that absolutely anything is possible when we put our minds to it and have the right perspective.

You can possess all the talent and skills in the world, but if you don't have the right attitude and mindset, you will always fall short of your best. Lou Holtz once said, *"Ability is what you're capable of doing. Motivation determines what you do. Attitude determines how well you do it."*

Let's face it, it's easy to be good on your good days. When everything clicks, it feels right. But what makes a Champion is their ability to remain in a positive frame of mind when things don't go to plan. Champions remain confident, optimistic, and hopeful, even in the direst situations. In contrast, athletes with negative attitudes become more pessimistic and typically expect the worst outcomes in tough situations. They complain about always being unlucky and have a *'why me?'* mentality. They revert to unhelpful thinking patterns and counter-productive habits.

Champions take the lessons from a defeat or tough loss and keep a positive attitude, which is not always easy to do. *You never lose, you learn.* The first step to overcoming failure is to accept it. For a Champion, the word *FAIL* stands for: *First Action In Learning.* They believe that by coming to terms with the reality in front of you, you become enabled to embrace it and work towards making things better. Champions believe this is the best way to progress and improve.

In my experience, I can't tell you the number of times I've witnessed an athlete or team come back from an almost certain defeat. The main reason this happens is because of their attitude and mindset. Champions are made during moments of pressure and adversity. When most athletes prefer to give up and feel sorry for themselves, Champions dig deep and use their mental toughness to keep persevering.

Excellence is an attitude. Without the right attitude, excellence isn't obtainable. Pat Riley, the former Miami Heat head coach, once said, *"If you have a positive attitude and constantly strive to give your best effort, eventually you will overcome your immediate problems and find you are ready for greater challenges."* Champions choose a winning mindset and keep persevering.

When you have the right attitude, you:

- Bring your best effort
- Don't make excuses
- Stay optimistic
- Bring a good energy

- Keep a good focus
- Take accountability
- Look for solutions
- Are grateful for all things

Champions have developed the habit and mindset of remaining positive under adversity. As W. Clement Stone once said, *"There is little difference in people, but that little difference makes a big difference. The little difference is attitude. The big difference is whether it is positive or negative."*

With the right attitude and mindset anything is possible.

Your skills are the entry ticket. Your attitude determines how far you go.

HABIT 23

THE HABIT OF SELF-DISCIPLINE

*"Once you have commitment, you need the discipline,
hard work and perseverance to get you there."*

– Haile Gebrselassie

The ability to accomplish great things comes down to how disciplined and committed you are to doing what is required. Author Harvey MacKay said, *"It doesn't matter whether you are pursuing success in business, sports, the arts, or life in general - the bridge between wishing and accomplishing is discipline."*

Anyone who has mastered a skill or craft hasn't achieved it without having a high level of self-discipline and commitment. I believe that, to succeed in sports, you need these three things:

1. A hunger and passion to succeed

2. The mindset to handle pressure

3. The self-discipline to do the hard stuff

Without a hunger and passion for what you do, it's almost impossible to become great at something. Without these two things, it's impossible to sustain the work and dedication required to succeed in the long run. Additionally, to be successful in a sport you must be able to control your emotions and remain positive under pressure. As Napoleon Hill said, *"Self-discipline begins with the mastery of thought. If you do not control your thoughts, you cannot control your needs."* And finally, having the self-discipline to put in the hard work, maintaining winning habits, and staying diligent to the small details, is vital to achieving your goals.

Passion + Mindset + Discipline = Success

News alert: Self-discipline is a skill that isn't flashy. In fact, it is a skill that often goes without being noticed. That moment of brilliance you witness from a world-class athlete or performer isn't luck. It's a result of the monomaniacal focus and discipline that's been put into thousands of hours practicing away from the cameras and crowds.

If you asked any Champion about how they achieved their success, one of the first things they'll say is, *'self-discipline.'* They will tell you that, without it, they wouldn't have reached the levels they did. Self-discipline puts you in the driver's seat. It's what keeps you focused on your goals and purpose, much like a camera lens zooming into a single object. The details and distractions around it dissipate as you zoom in.

Whilst on the subject of *being in the driver's seat*, it was in an interview with British Formula 1 Race Car driver, George Russell, where he said, *"My goal is to be a World Champion one day and to achieve that in this sport, it's all about staying disciplined, getting your priorities right, and giving it everything you've got."*

Champions understand that achieving anything of significance requires a high level of commitment and self-discipline. Excellence doesn't come from doing easy or average work. It comes from a willingness to do the uncomfortable and hard stuff.

You can either suffer the pain of discipline or suffer the pain of regret—the choice is yours. Discipline is not punishment. Discipline is what's needed to achieve excellence. Discipline is what eventually rewards you with choice. It's true that, in life, the more you discipline yourself, the easier life becomes.

The level of success you achieve will be determined by the level of your discipline and commitment. Champions have built the habit of self-discipline over the years. They know that without it, excellence isn't obtainable.

Excuses make today easy,
but tomorrow hard.
Discipline makes today hard,
but tomorrow easy.

HABIT 24

THE HABIT OF ASKING FOR FEEDBACK

*"Average players want to be left alone.
Good players want to be coached. Great players want
to be told the truth."*

– Doc Rivers

NBA Basketball Champion, Steph Curry, said, *"I want a coach to tell me what I need to improve, otherwise how am I going to get better?"* Let me ask you, as an athlete, are you proactive in asking for feedback? And, if so, what actions do you take after receiving it? Like Steph Curry, Champions want to be told the truth.

Let's admit it, we all love to receive positive feedback and compliments. Hearing these things helps boost our confidence and gives us a feeling of pride and accomplishment. However, the feedback that improves us is the kind we might not always want to particularly hear.

Having achieved much success at the University of Connecticut (UConn Basketball) spanning over almost four decades, Geno Auriemma was also the Head Coach to the USA Women's Olympic team. When it comes to feedback and criticism, Geno believes that *"those not willing to be criticized aren't willing to get better."* Geno is a firm believer that players who are not open to being coached and taking feedback (good or bad), stand little to no chance of playing in the teams he coaches.

Even though it may feel harsh or judgmental, feedback is crucial to your growth, learning, and development. Sam Ward, a professional Field Hockey player who has represented Great Britain at the Olympic and Commonwealth Games, said, *"Sometimes when you get feedback or criticism it can make you flinch at first, but when you take the time to digest it and understand that the person who gave it to you has good intent, you are then given the opportunity to improve and get better."*

When you change your relationship with how you view feedback, you open up a whole new world of learning and growth for yourself. Feedback is critical to your progress and learning. **When you are proactive and ask for feedback regularly, you accelerate the learning process even quicker.** It's important to remember that there is a difference between being teachable and coachable. When you are teachable, you follow instructions well. When you are coachable, you not only follow instructions well but are also proactive in seeking feedback and taking action.

One of Japan's most successful Figure Skaters is Yuzuru Hanyu, a 2x Olympic and double World Champion. He is known for his courage to attempt difficult jumps and for his exceptional performance routines on the ice. In an interview with a former coach from Yuzuru's youth days, he described Yuzuru as *"an athlete who worked hard, was insanely passionate about the sport, and someone who was always eager to receive feedback and learn."*

For feedback to be effective and useful, it hinges on it being timely, specific, and honest. When it comes to the timing of feedback, you might not always be in the right frame of mind, especially when frustrated or annoyed, but this can be the best time to learn and grow as an athlete. I discovered that, as a coach, the athletes who didn't accept or deal with feedback well were usually the ones who didn't progress as quickly. They inhibited their ability to learn and grow.

One last suggestion: When you ask for feedback, give your full attention to the person sharing it. Listen intently and don't interrupt. You might not always agree with the feedback, but always be respectful and thank the person who gave it. Remember, Champions and high performers don't wait for feedback, they ask for it!

Surround yourself with people who believe in you and tell you what you need to hear, not only what you want you to hear. Value these kinds of people because they are willing to tell you the truth.

HABIT 25

THE HABIT OF BEING A GREAT TEAM PLAYER

"The strength of the team is each individual member.
The strength of each member is the team."

– Phil Jackson

Many things constitute a great team player. When I think of a great team player, I immediately think of someone who adds value. I think of someone who is selfless and collaborates well with others. I think of someone who puts the team before themselves. Even when not a starter, a great team player supports loudly from the bench and encourages their fellow teammates in every way possible.

A great example of this comes from Gymnast, Ellie Black, who became Canada's most decorated female Pan Am gymnast after winning an incredible five medals at the 2019 Pan Am Games. However, it wasn't Ellie's performances on the floor that captured the fans attention; instead it was her performance on the sidelines. During the floor event, Black had landed in 3rd position and was eyeing a bronze medal until fellow Canadian teammate and competitor, Brooklyn Moors, completed a gold medal winning floor routine that pushed Black into 4th place. Onlookers observed Black cheering on Moors throughout her performance and embracing her with a big hug when her gold medal winning score was announced. When asked about her thoughts, Black dismissed any disappointment about missing out on the bronze medal. *"I was really excited for Brooklyn,"* Black said. *"I wasn't really thinking about myself. I was thinking about her."*

Austin Bayles, a Grand World Champion in Cheer-leading and a star of the Netflix show, *'Cheer'* describes a great team player like this: *"A great team player recognizes that success of the team is greater than themselves and they will find ways to bring value to the team even if they're not the star player."* If we look at past and present successful teams, a commonality that sticks out is that they all comprise of highly competent leaders and individuals. A great team player is not always the superstar player, the leading goal scorer, or the player who puts the most points on the scoreboard. Instead they are the ones aiming to make those around them better. Considered as one of the best Quarterbacks, Peyton Manning, said, *"The most valuable player makes the most players valuable."*

It's also important to note that coaches and leaders seek people who listen, collaborate well, and don't let their ego get in the way. Any coach will agree that when you commit to being a better person and teammate, you increase your value within the team.

10 Qualities of a Great Team Player:

1. Great teammates have humility. They are grateful and stay humble. They celebrate their teammates successes

2. Great teammates are selfless. They put the goals of the team above their own. They play any role asked of them

3. Great team players have a strong work ethic. They put in the extra work without having to be asked

4. Great team players bring high energy. They are positive and don't allow for negativity

5. Great team players are respectful. They treat others the way they would like to be treated

6. Great team players collaborate well. They understand that good chemistry is vital to having a healthy environment

7. Great team players are self-motivated. They are passionate and inspire others around them

8. Great team players are disciplined. They commit to winning habits and routines

9. Great team players are supportive. They elevate and lift others up

10. Great team players lead by example. They display the traits and characteristics that promote a positive team culture and environment

Aim to develop the habit of adding value to others, then watch how much your own value increases as a team player. As John Calipari, the University of Kentucky men's Basketball coach says: *"What type of teammates do you want to play with? Be that teammate yourself."*

> *"A player who makes a team great is more important than a great player."*
> **– John Wooden**

HABIT 26

THE HABIT OF
ALWAYS COMPETING HARD

"A successful competition for me is always going out there and putting 100 percent into whatever I'm doing."
– Simone Biles

With fierce competitors, few athletes could match the intensity and dogged determination of Tennis ace, Serena Williams. Facing the 23x Grand Slam Champion must have been one of sports toughest challenges for any opponent. Every time she stepped out to play, and no matter who her opponent was that day, Serena always fought her hardest and competed like a Champion. It's fair to say, she left it all out on the court.

When Serena was asked in an interview what she felt was one key to her success, the 4x Olympic gold medalist said, "*I think my greatest strength as a player is probably my mental game. Yes, I have a good serve. Yes, I have speed, good forehand, backhand. But all that would be nothing if I wasn't ready and prepared mentally to play every game, every match."*

Like Serena, Champions are Champions because of their tenacious determination and relentlessness in never quitting or throwing in the towel. No matter what the score or how dire the situation may be, they compete until the very end. It's also a known fact that Champions hate to lose more than they love to win.

Formula 1 World Champion, Max Verstappen, is another example of this mentality. In a season that can sometimes involve as much as 24 races, the key to winning a championship is about consistency and competing hard. Max said, *"I might not be able to win every race, but I will always compete hard until the end. It's all about scoring points every single race, even when it's not your day."* These words not only reflect a growth mindset, but a mentality that, even if you aren't going to be the winner that day, you still believe you have a chance of winning. The mentality of a Champion is that they always believe they can win.

To become a mentally tough competitor, one must learn and adopt the mindset of a Champion. Champions believe that, to become a tough competitor, practice time should be tougher than when they compete. This is something one of the world's best Badminton players, Pusarla Venkata Sindhu from India believes. A World Champion and Olympic medalist in the sport, Pusarla said, *"The greatest asset is a strong mind. If I know someone is training harder than I am, I have no excuses."*

Champions like Pusarla understand that the habits you build in practice become your habits under pressure come game time. As the goal of competition is about performing at your best, training might be more challenging and demanding than any competition could ever be. This is also something world famous Football coach, Pep Guardiola endorses. In his words, *"You play at the rhythm you train at. If you train badly, you play badly. If you work like a beast in training, you play the same way".*

Remember, the only factors fully under your control are your attitude, effort, and focus. Win or lose, when you know you gave it your all, it is easier to accept defeat or an unfavorable outcome. Giving your all doesn't always guarantee victory, but it leads to performing your best and having little regret over the result. Trust me, there is no worse regret than knowing you didn't give it your all. Champions don't always win. Champions are the ones who never quit trying.

Aim to become a competitor that others dread facing. Become an opponent feared by others - that feeling of dread washes over them when they see your name in the tournament draw. Build the reputation of being a stubborn opponent and someone who never throws in the towel, no matter what. This mindset doesn't require a special talent, only a choice.

Champions don't show up to get everything they want. They show up to give everything they have.

HABIT 27

THE HABIT OF MAKING YOUR BED

"If you want to change the world, start off by making your bed."
– Admiral William H. McRaven

As a young boy growing up, my parents would tell me to make my bed in the morning. Like any other kid, making my bed felt like a chore and not something I particularly enjoyed or wanted to do. I clearly didn't understand the importance of it back then, but little did I know that, by adhering to this one simple task, first thing in the morning, I was setting myself up for long term success.

It was at a University of Texas commencement speech back in 2014 given by Admiral William H. McRaven where he spoke about making your own bed. In what is now a universally well-known address, the Admiral encouraged the students to wake up each morning with a mindset of making the world a better place. He said:

> *"If you make your bed each morning, you will have accomplished your first task of the day. It will give you a small sense of pride and it will encourage you to do another task and another and another. By the end of the day, that one task completed will have turned into many tasks completed. Making your bed will also reinforce the fact that little things in life matter. If you can't do little things right, you will never do the big things right."*

During Admiral McRaven's Navy Seal training days, which entailed six months of runs in the sand, treading water, obstacles courses, unending calisthenics, and continuous harassment by veterans, one of the most valuable lessons he learned was the importance of making his bed. As you can imagine, being in the Navy Seals, he had to make his bed to perfection every morning. If he failed to, then there would be obvious ramifications. In fact, even after he sustained a serious injury, McRaven spent many months lying on a hospital bed wheeled into his government quarters. When he finally stood up unaided, the first thing he did was adjust his bed. It was his way of showing he was recovering and moving forward.

By making your bed, you have reinforced that the little things in life matter. You've made a disciplined choice. **Without discipline, it's impossible to achieve success whether it's in your personal or professional life.** How you do anything is how you do everything!

5 benefits to making your bed in the morning:

1. You accomplish your first task of the day
2. You take pride in your space
3. You take ownership of your day
4. It leads to more productivity
5. You come home to an already made bed

I know this might sound kind of funny, but I always feel proud of myself when I make my bed in the morning. I'll even say to myself: *"Good job Allistair.*

That's the first act of discipline achieved for the day!" Even though it's just as easy and convenient to have my bed made up by someone else (like in a hotel for example), I still prefer to make it myself. Making my bed makes me feel empowered, and I can't think of any better way to start the day.

Successful people have developed winning habits. Start your day with the habit of making your bed. It's your first act of discipline of the day. Remember that every single habit, big or small, will not only impact your day, but also your future.

Discipline can be defined as doing what needs to be done even when you don't feel like doing it.

HABIT 28

THE HABIT OF RECOVERING WELL

*"There is virtue in work and there is virtue in rest.
Use both and overlook neither."*

– Alan Cohen

As a former professional Duathlete who competed in five World Championships and over 200 professional races around the globe, I thrived on believing I was the hardest worker in my sport. I would find great pleasure in knowing I had trained longer and harder than my competitors or training partners. Sometimes, after being out on a training ride for more than four hours with other athletes, I would still want to add on at least another 30 mins to know I did more. However, the downside to that was that I would sometimes overtrain, with the result ending up as an injury or catching an illness.

In hindsight, I believe that, by not listening to my body, not resting, and not recovering enough, I jeopardized achieving my full potential. I didn't respect the value of rest and recovery enough. I believed that, if I wasn't always training, I was losing ground on my competitors. What I didn't realize was that I was over-training most of the time. Now days, they have hi-tech apps and watches to track all of this. But looking back, I wasn't just physically tired most of the time but also mentally tired. This ultimately led to low energy, mood swings, and severe fatigue. The bottom line is that I didn't understand the importance of recovery.

One of the greatest athletes and Basketball players of all time was Kobe Bryant. I remember a conversation I had with his athletic trainer at the LA Lakers where he told me that Kobe would dedicate two hours a day to his recovery. Before practice he would even do a pre-warm up (his own warm up routine before the team warm up). Even though Kobe loved to work hard, he knew when to take a day off to rest and avoid overtraining. Mambo, as he was known, understood the importance of recovering and taking proper care of his body.

Paying attention to things such as taking proper rest, nutrition, sleep, and hydration are underappreciated and under-utilized training variables critical to your performance, health, and injury prevention. A lack of proper recovery will not only prevent you from reaching your goals but will more than likely hurt your performance. When you consistently stress your system and don't give it adequate time to recover, you risk experiencing:

- Fatigue
- A loss of appetite/weight loss
- Decreased motivation
- Illness and a weakened immune system
- Frequent injuries
- Trouble sleeping

The Portuguese Football star, Cristiano Ronaldo, regarded as one of the fittest athletes of all time, even had a high-tech regeneration room installed in his home. Before leaving his house for practice, he would prepare his body for the work ahead. On returning home, he again would utilize his home regeneration facility to aid his recovery.

When it comes to performing at a high level, proper rest and recovery are the most important factors to achieving your potential. Avoid becoming a slave to what your training program says. Instead, pay attention and listen closely to what your body is telling you.

Hard Work + Rest = Success

As an athlete, it's important that you learn how to listen to your body. Know when to push yourself and know when to back off and give your body rest. Sometimes, a break from your routine is the thing you need.

If you want to change your outcomes, start by changing your habits.

HABIT 29

THE HABIT OF KEEPING IT SIMPLE

"Keep it simple, when you get too complex
you forget the obvious."

– Al McGuire

A high performing athlete is not only well prepared physically, technically, and strategically,
but someone in control of their emotions and
who keeps a cool head under pressure. One of the best
lessons you can learn in life is mastering how to remain
calm. The Chinese philosopher Lao Tzu said, *"Mastering
others is strength, mastering yourself is true power."*

I vividly remember a conversation I had with an
Olympic Volleyball coach a few years ago in Malibu,
California. I wanted to know what advice he gave his
athletes for handling the pressure moments during
competition. He advised his athletes to always get back
to the basics and keep things simple. He mentioned that

we tend to overthink and complicate things when pressure builds.

Under adversity, Champions always revert to keeping things simple and not overthinking it. A great example of this comes from the former Olympic 100m record holder, Carl Lewis. He said, *"My thoughts before a big race are usually very simple. I tell myself: Get out of the blocks, run your race, stay relaxed. If you run your race, you'll win. Channel your energy. Focus."*

You will hardly ever see a Champion look flustered or panicked. For example, think of Roger Federer or Tom Brady. Even under intense circumstances, they remain calm and in control of their emotions. They can slow the things happening around them down. Like a captain of a ship navigating their way through stormy waters, they bring calm to the storm.

Try to think back to your most memorable and best performances. What are the commonalities to each occasion? What do you recall as the most important factors or ingredients that led to those great performances? My guess is that it almost felt effortless, you kept things simple, were in the zone, and focused on the process. I remember reading a quote from Olympic Snowboard Champion, Shaun White. When asked how to describe what it felt like when he performed at his best, he said, *"At that point, you really aren't thinking. You're just letting it happen. It's a mixture of being focused then slightly not caring."*

Another great piece of advice I received for performing under pressure was from a Diving coach based in Australia. She mentioned that an athlete should try not to have more than one or two things to focus on when competing. Any more than that is information overload. She mentioned that, in competition, an athlete's nerves and anxiety levels are increased, so it's harder to absorb information. When we keep things simple, we remember strategies and tactics easier. This helps the athlete perform at a higher level.

As an athlete, when you have mental clarity, your mind isn't clouded with indecision, what-ifs, complexity, or worry. Under pressure situations, a free mind isn't concerned about what could go wrong because those thoughts don't have time to cross your mind.

You might have come across the KISS principle. KISS is an acronym for *Keep It Simple, Stupid.* I tweaked this slightly for the athletes (and coaches) I work with, preferring to go by: *Keep It Short & Simple.*

Keeping things simple is a great way to keep your mind clear, not that you can't handle complicated subjects. In fact, finding the simple way to do things is a sign of intelligence. As Albert Einstein once said, *"Out of complexity, find simplicity."*

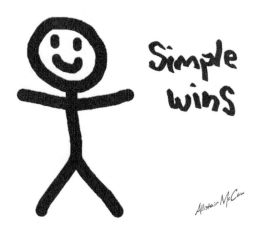

*Aim to keep things simple.
It's the overthinking
that kills you in the end.*

.

HABIT 30

THE HABIT OF MAXIMIZING YOUR STRENGTHS

"Success comes by strengthening your strengths more than improving on your weaknesses. If you can maximize the potential of your strength, then you become a Champion."

– Dr. Lucas D. Shallua

O ne of the greatest assets we have is the ability to continually improve and learn about ourselves. Through the self-examination process required to discover where our strengths and weaknesses lie, we gain better knowledge and insight into who we are, not just as an athlete, but as a person, which increases our level of self-awareness.

As an athlete, it's crucial that you know your strengths. Do you know yours? Knowing and utilizing your strengths is probably one of the most important contributors to your success. They are usually easy to identify because it's something you love to do and are good at. Ask any Champion what their favorite play, stroke or shot is, and they will tell you their strength. Their strengths are their weapons and what help them win.

Author and researcher, Tom Rath said, *"When we build on our strengths and daily successes - instead of focusing on failures - we simply learn more."* I've discovered that many athletes spend too much time fixated on their weaknesses instead of their strengths. The danger in this is that the athlete places too much time, focus, and attention on their limiting factors. When this happens, they deplete their self-belief and confidence.

We are all unique and have our different strengths and weaknesses. It's one of the first questions I like to ask an athlete: *"What's your favorite play/stroke/shot?"* I believe this is an important question to ask, as it tells me what weapon gives them the most payback and adds to their confidence. I then like to ask how often they practice and work on it.

What I've discovered in observing Champions is that they spend most of their time polishing and refining their strengths. When Champions go to battle, they don't bring their knives and handguns; they instead bring out their heavy weaponry. Their game strategy is focused first around utilizing their strengths, then, by exploiting their opponents' weaknesses.

I once had the opportunity to work with a two-time Grand Slam Tennis Finalist who used to spend 80% of his practice time refining his two strengths: serve and forehand. These were what he called his 'money makers.' He had a successful professional career, but he was quick to remind me that, during his early development years, he spent countless hours working on his weaknesses.

The author, Marcus Buckingham quoted, *"You will only excel by maximizing on your strengths, never by fixating on your weaknesses."* It is important to note that, as you develop and progress throughout your career, more time is spent optimizing your strengths. Of course, that doesn't mean you neglect and ignore working on your weaknesses.

Identifying your strengths is essential for success. Know them and grow them. Champions capitalize on their strengths and manage their weaknesses. They build their confidence and self-belief from recognizing them. Without knowing how to acknowledge your strengths, you may waste a lot of time working on the wrong things.

Know your strengths – Identify them.
Grow your strengths – Practice them.
Maximize your strengths – Use them.

Champions draw confidence and self-belief from focusing on their strengths.

HABIT 31

THE HABIT OF LISTENING WELL

"When you talk, you are only repeating what you already know. But if you listen, you may learn something new."

– Dalai Lama

Mark Twain wisely said, *"Wisdom is the reward you get for a lifetime of listening when you would have rather talked."* Great listeners are teachable and coachable, so it comes as little surprise that every coach loves an athlete who listens and absorbs information well.

There is a difference between hearing and listening. Hearing revolves around the physiological act of perceiving sounds, whereas listening encompasses actively paying attention to the words and sounds that you hear to absorb their meaning.

When the former captain of the England National Cricket team, Kevin Pietersen, was asked in an interview what one of the most important life lessons he'd ever learned was. He said, *"You've got two ears and one mouth. Listen more than you speak."*

Listening is a skill set that often gets overlooked, not only in sports, but more important, in life. World class performers and leaders in their fields are great listeners. They don't only listen with their ears, but with all their senses, like the former three-time World Champion and #1 ranked Squash player in the world, Nick Matthew describes it. Nick, who has since retired from professional Squash, is now coaching and developing some of the game's best talent. I asked Nick what he saw in the more coachable players and those who developed and improved their game quicker. He said, *"The players who generally improve the quickest are those who are 100% present. As a coach, when you talk, they don't just listen with their ears, they also make eye contact, they have the right body language, and they are ready to implement the information you have given them."*

Poor listeners are usually either distracted, dis-interested or even worse, caught up in themselves and their ego. These athletes are prone to making more mistakes and errors that can eventually cost them or their team dearly.

Good listening skills lead to better learning skills, and better learning skills lead to better skill execution. What you learn and put into practice ultimately makes you a better athlete and student. The best listeners are those people who ask a lot of questions and put the answers into action literally. They question the details. They are eager to get better. It's obvious to say that the good listeners also learn faster.

Listening is a big part of being coachable. Another example of this comes from NBA Basketball player, Donovan Mitchell. When asked about listening, he said, *"I saw a lot of guys who I thought should have been stars, but they didn't listen…they were 10 times better than me; but they didn't listen…. they did things their own way and got cocky. In order for me to continue my success, I have to be someone who listens…. It may not always be what I want to hear, but it's the right thing that I need to hear."*

Some traits of a good listener include:

- You have an open mind and are eager to learn
- You don't interrupt the speaker
- You maintain eye contact and keep focused
- You request clarification on what's been said

As focusing on building and sharpening your game skills is important, so too is becoming a better listener. Remember, we don't learn from talking, we learn from listening. You only grow when you are open to learning and listening well.

*Listening is a big part of being coachable.
You will never maximize your potential
if you don't humble yourself and
learn to listen well.*

HABIT 32

THE HABIT OF ADHERING TO RITUALS

*"Pop finally convinced me a pre-shot routine was
necessary for consistency, and I've used the same one
ever since."*

– Tiger Woods

Whenever you observe Champions and elite performers, you would be excused for thinking they always look calm and in complete control of their emotions, thoughts, and feelings. Well, that's not always the case. According to Hope Solo, the former United States women's Soccer goalkeeper, *"Every athlete acquires routines to help control nerves."* They have conditioned themselves to be more self-aware of such things as their body language and behaviors.

Having been fortunate to be around many elite athletes, Champions also get nervous and feel butterflies in their stomach. They are human too. However, the biggest difference lies in how they control these feelings and one way they do this is by adhering to certain rituals and routines.

So, what are rituals? A ritual is a behavior or action an athlete regularly performs with the belief they have a specific power or influence to help their performance. To the onlooker, they may seem irrelevant or unimportant, but for the athlete, these patterns strongly influence their preparation and success in the competition arena. American Alpine Skier, Lindsay Vonn states, *"I have a race routine. I have a team of people helping me. I have winning habits. I have balance in my life."* This is her pattern for success.

Some pre-competition and in-game rituals can include such things as the time an athlete likes to arrive at the venue, how they warm-up, or what they like to eat before competing. They can also include how they prepare before a certain play during competition i.e., a Soccer player taking a penalty kick or a Baseball player pitching a ball. These are all designed to help prime the athlete's mind and body.

When you observe different sports at the professional level, you will notice that most athletes have set routines and rituals. Some examples include:

- Before a penalty kick, All Blacks Rugby player, Dan Carter takes a deep breath and then visualizes where he wants his kick to go

- NBA's, Steph Curry likes to sink a shot from the edge of the tunnel at the end of his warm up

- Before a Formula One race, Pierre Gasly likes to do some reaction drills with his Finnish trainer, Pyry Salmela, to sharpen his reflexes

- Multiple Grand Slam Tennis Champion, Rafael Nadal likes his water bottles placed a certain way. He also likes to towel himself after every point

Champion athletes use rituals to help themselves prepare before competing. It helps them enter a competitive mindset that best suits them for optimal performance. Former Formula 1 Champion, Jenson Button, mentioned that he would always follow a pre-race routine. Even if there was a restart due to a race incident, he would go through the exact same routine again before starting.

So, the next time you watch professional athletes go about their business, remember that, behind those acts of excellence and brilliance, are many 'hidden' rituals and routines. They have implemented these rituals and routines to help keep them in the present and in the right frame of mind.

Like the Champions, aim to develop the habit of implementing helpful rituals and routines into your game. Doing this will help you optimize your performance and influence positive outcomes.

"Having set rituals and routines allows me to focus and feel more comfortable before and during a game."

– Kevin Love

HABIT 33

THE HABIT OF SURROUNDING YOURSELF WITH THE RIGHT PEOPLE

"Surround yourself with good people. People who are going to be honest with you and look out for your best interests."

– Derek Jeter

"**S**how me your friends and I'll show you your future." In life, there can be no greater decision than choosing the environment you are in and the people you surround yourself with. People with a Champion-minded outlook in life gravitate toward like-minded people. In fact, it's been proven time and time again that the people you spend the most time with heavily influence your well-being and the direction of your future.

The great motivational speaker, Jim Rohn, once said, *"You're the average of the five people you spend the most time with."* Our actions and behaviors are heavily influenced by others. For example, if your friends like to hang out at parties, then there's a good chance you will do the same. If your friends are negative and pessimistic, then that can also have a detrimental influence on you. If your network exhibits a specific behavior, then your perception and behavior change. It takes me back to when my father always reminded me that *"you can't soar with the eagles if you hang around the turkeys"*.

If your goal is to become a Champion, then it only makes sense to be around people who have been a success themselves. Learn from them, observe them, ask questions, and absorb information. You can save a lot of time, effort, and money by getting the best advice and guidance.

Founder of Hintsa Performance, Dr. Aki Hintsa, said it best when it came to well-being. He said, *"Success is a by-product of well-being."* That's why it's important to make sure that you're spending time around people who are good for your well-being, challenge you to be better, and are supportive of your goals.

As an athlete, you want to surround yourself with those who:

- Tell you the truth
- Challenge you to be better
- Support and encourage you
- Treat you with respect
- Inspire you to achieve excellence
- Are there for you during the good and bad times

Many people gravitate towards those who only sing their praises and tell them how amazing they are. This unfortunately leads to a sense of entitlement and distorted self-image. We need to be careful of spending too much time with those who don't have our best interests at heart. Remember that there is a big difference between the people who tell you what you like to hear and the people who tell you what you need to hear. Gravitate towards the latter.

Aim to distance yourself from:

- The energy vampires
- The gossipers
- The trollers and haters
- Those with no ambitions to improve
- Those who are jealous of your success

It's healthy to be surrounded by people who can provide you with honest, authentic feedback. Find people who have your best interests at heart and see the potential in you. Find people who applaud your wins but are still there to support you when you fail. It will enable you to establish a balanced view of yourself.

The people we choose to surround ourselves with either raise our standards or lower them.
Choose wisely.

HABIT 34

THE HABIT OF EMBRACING REPETITION

"It's the repetition of affirmations that leads to belief. And once that belief becomes a deep conviction, things begin to happen."

– Muhammed Ali

Many athletes love the idea of becoming great at their chosen sport. But how many will endure the countless hours and sometimes tedious work it takes to get there? The next time you watch a world-class athlete in action, you can be sure of one thing: they have spent many years practicing the same basic movements repeatedly to get to where they are today.

Daniel Cornier, a former UFC Light Heavyweight Champion and former Olympic Wrestler, understood what it would take to get to the top of his sport. He said,

"You don't get to the highest levels in the sport without having the basics in order, and there's only one way to improve the basics – through repetition."

A commonality I've observed in Champion performers is that they have a totally different relationship with practice. They have a deeper understanding of what it takes to become elite. They have learned to value feedback and countless hours of focused repetition needed to achieve excellence. Champions understand that if you want to master a skill or habit, the key is to start with repetition, not perfection.

Martial arts demands high focus and repetition. Choi Hong Hi, regarded as the founder of Taekwondo and one of the greatest Martial artists, once said, *"To become an expert at Taekwondo you first have to master the most basic movements and fundamentals. And to be able to master anything, repetition is required."* Bruce Lee, the iconic Martial Arts expert, was renowned for his physical fitness and vigor through a dedicated fitness regimen. Amongst many other incredible abilities, Lee could punch an astonishing nine times in one second, while his one-inch punch could force a 75kg opponent five to six meters away - now, that's what you call power! When asked how he achieved such incredible feats, Lee famously said, *"I fear not the man who has practiced 10,000 kicks once, but I fear the man who has practiced one kick 10,000 times."*

When it comes to the sports science side of things, repetition has proven to have incredible effects on the brain. It makes our "wires" stronger, faster, and more accurate. The best athletes focus on perfect effort instead of perfect practice. They understand that, by focusing on the basics and the process of repetition, they refine their expertise and increase their chances of success.

Think of anyone who has achieved success in their field: Ed Sheeran, Sachin Tendulkar, Ariana Grande, Trischa Zorn, Erling Haaland, Chen Meng, Irene Van Dyk, or Wayne Gretzky, and they will tell you that the path to greatness involves embracing repetition. It was well known that Kobe Bryant would get at least 400 shots in before his team practice even started! These icons spent countless hours, over numerous years, performing the same routines, exercises, drills, and skills repeatedly to become the best in their chosen fields.

The best athletes make fewer mistakes because they understand that repetition is the greatest error-reducer. Champions don't practice until they get it right, they practice until they don't get it wrong. The ability to handle this repetitiveness or what some may call 'the boring stuff' is actually a mental strength. Mentally strong athletes can keep focus long after the rest have checked out. It's one of the key reasons why they go onto to achieve greater things.

The way you think is a habit, and like any other habit, it can be changed.
It just requires practice and repetition.

HABIT 35

THE HABIT OF TAKING DAYTIME NAPS

"Sleep is extremely important to me – I need to rest and recover for the training I do to be absorbed by my body."

– Usain Bolt

Performing at a high level requires having the right balance of work, rest, and recovery. Many studies prove that taking naps throughout the day can have a profound effect on an athlete's level of alertness and performance.

Champions understand the importance of taking naps because, when we're resting or asleep, our bodies are repairing muscle tissue, topping up stamina levels, and helping us regain general awareness. In a study carried out by the Harvard Medical School, it was found that taking a short nap can reinforce the memory of what was learned. This is also true of a full night's sleep.

Olympian and Greek professional Runner, Alexi Pappas, has learned that finding balance is the key to successful training. She believes that sleep and recovery are as important as her running workouts. She said, *"I've grown to take my nap time as seriously as I take my runs. In fact, I have even started calling my daytime naps my 'second practice' of the day."*

A short, 20-minute nap during the day can be beneficial to athletes. Like Pappas, Steve Nash, a former two-time NBA MVP of the game, understands the value of sleep and taking daytime naps. With his performance and recovery, Nash said, *"Diet and sleep are probably the two biggest tools to recover, and it's definitely something that's hard to do when you're traveling a lot. I like to nap almost every day as it helps with my recovery and alertness."* Other well-known athletes who are advocates of taking daytime naps include Tijana Boskovic, Aleksander Sapic, Ryan Hall, and Son Heung-Min.

5 Benefits of Taking a Daytime Nap:

1. Improves mood
2. More energy
3. Increases mental alertness
4. Helps with muscle alertness
5. Boosts the immune system

In nearly every sport, taking naps is now considered a key component and necessity to achieving peak performance. Today, we even find professional sports teams and colleges with state-of-the-art purpose-built sleep rooms at their training facilities for their players to recover during the day. Many teams even recruit "sleep coaches" to help their players snooze better.

5 Tips for Taking Effective Naps:

1. Aim to take a nap after lunchtime between 1pm and 3pm, when according to science our body naturally feels tired
2. Go to a quiet place with no noise or distractions

3. Turn off all electronics

4. Make sure your room is dark, close the shutters, or get dark curtains because a bright room can affect your sleep quality

5. After your nap, aim to have a glass of water to rehydrate

It has been scientifically proven that a nap before a practice session improves cognitive performance and subjective alertness and fatigue. It helps to restore physical and mental freshness, getting close to the levels of performance one would get with a full night's sleep, and boosts morale for the rest of the day. Personally, I've witnessed the benefits of the athletes I've worked with who take naps during the day, especially with their moods and energy levels. The connection between how well-rested an athlete is and their physical and cognitive performance is undisputed.

Develop the habit of incorporating a nap into your daily schedule. It will help provide you with the energy and alertness to finish your day strong!

To stay sharp, focused and energized, Champions take daytime naps to recharge their batteries.

HABIT 36

THE HABIT OF STAYING FOCUSED

*"It's not the number of hours you practice.
It's about the number of hours your mind is present
during the practice."*

– Kobe Bryant

When it comes to sports, one of the greatest obstacles of an athlete's game is loss of focus. Champions can eliminate distractions and stay focused on what matters. If two athletes have equal skill and ability, it is almost certain that the one able to best focus on the task at hand will prevail.

All the best athletes in the world can concentrate and block distractions. It reminds me of the time I attended an Archery practice at the United States Olympic training facility in Chula Vista, California. During a break from working with another team that day, I stopped by their facility to observe some of the National level athletes at work. Archery demands precision, control, mental calmness, and most of all, focus. Admiring the caliber of athletes there, I was blown away by how they were able to lock in on their target, focus on their form, and ignore the distraction and noises around them. It was a masterclass in deep focus and concentration.

Mental focus is one of the key traits of a Champion. Focus is the ability to shut out whatever is going on around you and be 100% mentally locked into what you are doing in the present moment. Champions excel because of their ability to quickly move on after an error or mistake and redirect their attention to the next play. This is something Finnish Ice Hockey Olympian, Michelle Karvinen, believes is key to becoming a Champion. Seen as one of the best technical players in the world, she said, *"I don't think I've ever won any game without making mistakes. It's about having the mental strength to get over mistakes quickly and re-focus. This is one thing you must master to become a great player."* It is a powerful shift for any athlete when they realize they can control where they place their attention.

A critical mental performance skill of any athlete is having a deep concentration and focus, not only during competition time but also during practice time. Learning how to become a more focused athlete involves experimenting and occasionally training with intentional distractions. One of the greatest Golfers to ever play the game, Tiger Woods, implemented this strategy by practicing his golf swing while his father, Earl, would jingle keys or drop coins to make a noise.

Olympic Gymnast and gold medalist, Shannon Miller, once said, "*In the Olympic Games, everyone is talented. Everyone trains hard. Everyone does the work. What separates the gold medalists from the silver medalists is simply the mental game.*" When an athlete mentions the mental game, he or she is referring to the ability to have mental focus.

When I asked one of the world's best female Squash players, Amanda Sobhy, what advice she would give when it came to keeping focus as an athlete, she replied, "*Keeping focus is about staying present and keeping it very simple. Staying present in the moment is key whether it's focusing on your breath or having a cue word or mantra.*"

To be the best version of yourself and achieve optimal performance, it's critical that you develop the habits and skills of staying focused and in the moment. Determine your priorities and focus on them. The more you practice focus, the more it becomes a habit.

You don't get results by focusing on results. You get results by focusing on the habits and behaviors that produce results.

HABIT 37

THE HABIT OF
DEVELOPING GRIT & RESILIENCE

*"Adversity, if you allow it to, will fortify you and
make you the best you can be."*

– Kerri Walsh Jennings

Grapes must be crushed to create wine. Olives are pressed to get oil. Diamonds are formed under pressure. Seeds grow in the dark. Every Champion understands, *'to become a Champion, you need to be willing to embrace pressure and the more difficult moments. If it doesn't challenge you, it doesn't change you.'*

Mentally tough athletes embrace the challenges that come their way. When faced with adversity, they take responsibility. It's a known fact that coaches and recruiters name grit and resilience as two of the most important qualities they seek in an athlete. Veteran NFL coach, Pete Carroll, a winning Super Bowl coach of the Seattle Seahawks, admits these two attributes are key when he looks at recruiting new players for his team. Like Carroll, many coaches acknowledge that talent and skills can be taught, but not without grit as the foundation.

It's easy to recognize an athlete who has grit and resilience. When things get tough, they don't point fingers at others, blame or complain. When pressure and the more challenging moments arrive, they embrace them with strength and courage. Athletes with grit and resilience have an ability to endure, push beyond their physical limits and do whatever it takes.

The ability to overcome setbacks and persevere is a key component in helping Champions achieve their goals. It's a question I posed to Bob Bowman, the longtime coach of

Olympic Swimming Champion, Michael Phelps. When it comes to resilience, Bowman believes that it's something that you're not born with. It must be earned, then nurtured. Behavioral psychologist, Angela Duckworth, explains grit:

> *"We define grit as perseverance and passion for long-term goals. Grit entails working strenuously toward challenges, maintaining effort and interest over years despite failure, adversity, and plateaus in progress. The gritty individual approaches achievement as a marathon; his or her advantage is stamina. Whereas disappointment or boredom signals to others that it is time to change trajectory and cut losses, the gritty individual stays the course."*

Grit and resilience can be developed when:

- You adopt the right attitude and mindset
- You take the hard path instead of the easy way out
- You don't complain or make excuses when things get hard

- You embrace the challenges and difficulties

- You view setbacks as opportunities for growth

Grit and resilience are important characteristics in becoming a Champion, not only in sports, but more important, in life. Along the journey, some will doubt you and you will fail occasionally, but if you respond with an attitude of positivity and determination, you will eventually succeed.

Remember that, in life, it's not how far you fall, it's about how high you bounce back. Even when someone doubts you or doesn't believe in you, use that as fuel and motivation not to prove them wrong, but to prove to yourself that you had it in you all along.

Champions have adopted the habit of not shying away from the uncomfortable. They embrace the obstacles, challenges, and setbacks. They understand that, when you adopt this approach and mindset, the reward is obtaining more grit and resilience. Hard work might make you good, but grit will make you great.

Your level of grit and resilience will define you more than your wins and losses do.

HABIT 38

THE HABIT OF EVOLVING

*"There is no way around hard work. Embrace it.
You have to put in the hours because there's always
something which you can improve."*

– Roger Federer

They say that the only constant in life is change. As an athlete, if you aren't willing to change and adapt, you eventually get figured out by the competition and left behind. One of the main reasons Champions are Champions is because of their ability to stay curious and open-minded to improving their skills. Your ability to grow and succeed starts with your willingness to metamorphosize and evolve.

Champions and high performers never stand still. They are always evolving. No matter how great they become, they are continuously looking for ways to improve themselves. A Champion knows that, periodically, they need to reinvent themselves to stay ahead of the competition. This plays a big part in their motivation.

A habit the best athletes focus on to improve their skills is to seek the best advice. These individuals will usually have experienced people in their corner they receive advice from and like to share ideas with. They seek people that have been where they want to be. They know that success is never achieved alone; it involves a team of people.

As an athlete, when you think you've arrived, you're done. You never 'arrive'. There is no finish line to what your potential is. That's the whole beauty of it because you can always improve. A few years ago, I was working with a professional athlete during her off-season in Dubai. On the court next to us was none other than Roger Federer, one of the greatest Tennis players of all time. Roger was the then ranked #1 in the world and had won 17 Grand Slam titles (he would win three more in his career). Being on the court next to him for over two weeks, I got to witness a genius and sporting icon at work.

Besides admiring Roger's poetry-like movement around the court and flawless technique when striking a ball, what stood out to me most was the feedback and information being shared between him and his team. During his practices, I would overhear Roger and his team discussing elements about his game and where they felt he could still improve. It was inspiring to witness the world's best Tennis player still hungry to improve and get even better.

In the last few years of his career, with Roger being in his mid to late 30's, he knew that, to still compete at the highest level, he had to evolve as a player and tweak certain parts of his game. That's what prompted him to hire the services of former Croatian professional player, Ivan Ljubicic, as his coach to help him re-invent his game and stay competitive against the best players in the world.

Like Roger, elite athletes and high performers at the top of their sport could so easily be satisfied with what they've already achieved, but here's the thing: they aren't. That's the difference between the best and the rest. No matter how great they become, the Champions want to continue improving and keep raising the bar.

Champions and high performers don't rest upon their laurels. They evolve and change before they must. They are aware that what might have worked last season doesn't necessarily mean it will work now. They know they need to keep evolving and adapting to stay on top of their game.

What about you? How are you evolving? How are you improving? Whom are you learning from and what steps are you taking? Don't mistakenly wait until it's too late to change. Find the right people, coaches, and mentors to help you develop, grow, and evolve. This is how you improve your performance and gain a mental edge.

Champions don't rest upon their laurels. They keep evolving to maintain a competitive edge.

HABIT 39

THE HABIT OF DOING THE EXTRA WORK

"I knew there were hundreds of thousands of kids doing the same thing, but I would do more than what anyone else was willing to do."

– Michael Phelps

Regarded as one of the greatest coaches in the history of British Football, former Manchester United manager, Sir Alex Ferguson once said, "*Hard work will always overcome natural talent when natural talent does not work hard enough*."

Champions don't need to be asked to do the extra work. They do it. They understand that excellence involves doing more than what's required. The simple life lesson of *'the more you put in, the more you get out'* is evident for those that repeatedly travel the extra mile.

Champions commit to that extra set of hill sprints when their legs and lungs feel like they are about to explode. They push through those extra reps in the gym when their muscles are screaming for them to stop. Committing to additional stretching after a long, hard session is never ignored. Putting in the extra work is a choice. It's a place where good becomes great and where the ordinary becomes extraordinary. It's a place where all Champions are made.

The New Zealand All Blacks Rugby team is one of the most successful sports teams in history, with an 80% win rate. One of the core principles in their culture has been the motto, *'Champions do extra'*. This philosophy simply means finding incremental ways to do more – be it in the gym, on the field, or simply for the team. The focus is on developing the habit of continual improvement, the creation of an ongoing learning environment, and a willingness to give their all for the jersey and their country.

It's not up to your coaches or parents to push you to work harder. To become your best and achieve your fullest potential, it must come from you.

No one will make you better. A coach can provide you with the tools, knowledge, and support, but in the end, you are the only one responsible for your development and progress.

I encourage you to introduce the habit of doing additional work. I promise you will reap the rewards. The bonus is that coaches love an athlete who shows commitment and a deep hunger to improve. It's all those little extra efforts you give daily that add up to bigger successes. Just think about it…

15 mins extra per day adds up to 91 hours in a year
30 mins extra per day adds up to 182 hours per year
45 mins extra per day adds up to 271 hours per year
60 mins extra per day adds up to 365 hours per year.

Remember that putting in the extra work isn't for everyone, but neither is winning. Hard work will make you good, but it's all the little extra efforts on top of the hard work that will make you great. Champions do more and give more to be more. They see value in doing the extra work. It's one of the main reasons they are Champions.

In the end, the number one underlying reason why the 5% succeed, be it in sports, business, or any other field for that matter, is because of this: They are willing to do more than what's been asked.

Never underestimate the importance of the small details and doing the extra work. The difference between victory and defeat can be a single point, a one hundredth of a second, or just a few millimeters.

HABIT 40

THE HABIT OF PRACTICING SELF-AWARENESS

"I think self-awareness is probably the most important thing toward being a Champion."

– Billie Jean King

Self-awareness is the starting point for development, change, and growth. As an athlete, if you lack self-awareness, it's almost impossible for you to be mentally tough or resilient. And we know that mental toughness and resilience are the cornerstones of athletic success.

Reading this book is a sure sign you are dedicated to self-improvement, personal development, and becoming the best you can be. Each day, through your choices, habits, and actions, you are either taking steps forwards or backwards.

No self-development can take place without self-awareness. As an athlete, the best way to improve yourself is to understand yourself better. This results in you learning more from each performance (good or bad). The American author Lawrence Bossidy once said, *"Self-awareness gives you the capacity to learn from your mistakes and your successes. It enables you to keep growing."*

When you are more self-aware, your strengths and weaknesses are clearer to you. It is often said that, if you don't have an awareness of something, you can't change it. Self-awareness doesn't stop you from making mistakes; instead, it allows you to learn from them. Having good self-awareness is an essential part of performing well. It's one of the key factors why Champions make better decisions and stay in control of their emotions.

When an athlete lacks self-awareness, they will struggle to regulate their own thoughts, feelings, and behaviors and assert self-control when needed. Under adverse and pressured situations, these athletes will usually default to unhelpful thoughts, habits, and patterns.

When an athlete has good self-awareness, they are more equipped to 'catch' themselves from falling into unhelpful habits or behaviors. The reason is that they recognize the thoughts and feelings earlier. Champions know that self-awareness is a superpower with mental toughness and consistency in performance.

Self-awareness is the first, and possibly, most important part of emotional intelligence. People with high emotional intelligence have a greater awareness with themselves (self-awareness) and other people (social awareness). Great leaders and team players are usually highly competent in both.

Energy is contagious, and nobody likes to be around a moody or negative person, but, by having a good level of self-awareness, you can energize your team through positive actions and emotions. Remember, you are always responsible for the energy you bring when you enter a room. Great teams include people mindful of this energy and hold it as a standard.

5 ways you can improve your self-awareness:

1. Be mindful of your strengths and weaknesses

2. Ask for feedback from your parents, coaches, and teammates

3. Keep track of things such as your self-talk, thoughts, and behaviors

4. Watch videos of your practices and matches and be on the lookout for things such as your body language and energy

5. Know your emotional triggers

I encourage you to practice more self-awareness in your life. To improve and grow, we must be more open and willing to look within ourselves and identify the areas we most need to change to become the athlete and person we wish to be.

Champions know that self-awareness is a superpower. It's a key component to mental toughness and consistency in performance.

HABIT 41

THE HABIT OF PAYING ATTENTION TO THE SMALL DETAILS

*"It's the little details that are vital.
Little things make big things happen."*

– John Wooden

There's a reason some athletes go on to greater things and some never reach expectations. Success favors those who are coachable and those who are willing to put in the work and go the extra mile. It's a lesson not only in sports but also in life.

The actor, Dwayne "The Rock" Johnson said, "*Success isn't overnight. It's when every day you get a little better than the day before. It all adds up.*" Once the highest paid male actor in Hollywood, Johnson understands how important hard work and the small details matter.

Everyone wants success, but not everyone will go through the processes that will ensure the highest chance of reaching that goal. The simple truth about paying attention to the small details is that they require more time, more effort, and demand more attention. That's why not everyone is willing or able to accomplish greatness.

Taking shortcuts rarely turns out well for those who want to reach a high level in the activity they participate in. Shortcuts are dangerous and can cost you dearly. Just think, how many times have we seen mistakes and epic failures occur because of poor preparation, faulty equipment, or inadequate planning?

A great example of paying attention to the small details comes from UCLA's John Wooden, a coach regarded as the greatest in NCAA history, winning 10 championships over 12 years. When asked by reporters what his secret was, he said, *"It all starts with your socks and your shoes."* Yep, you read that right!

Coach Wooden believed that the most important part of an athlete's equipment was their socks and shoes, especially if you played on a hard surface. First, he believed that a player should have the correct sized shoes and socks that properly fit.

The first day of practice at UCLA was always a day full of nerves and excitement, especially for the newer players on the team. As they waited for the arrival of Coach Wooden, each player wondered what secrets of the game they would learn and what game winning strategies they would be exposed to.

Instead, at the first practice, Coach Wooden would have all his players gather, some new and some who had been playing under him in previous seasons, and demonstrate how to put on a sock. The purpose of this was that he believed if a sock was not put on properly, a blister could occur. And if a player got a blister, then their practice and playing time could be affected.

Even though this basic exercise only took a few minutes, Coach Wooden believed that it was important enough to do at the beginning of every new season. After he was done with the socks, he would then demonstrate to his players how to properly tie their shoelaces. The rationale behind this was that if a shoelace came undone during a game, that 'mishap' could cost the team not only the game, but possibly even the Championship. Coach

Wooden believed that success was found in attention to the small details.

Having been around world class performers, I have seen with my own eyes how meticulous they are in their preparation. As Coach Wooden drilled into his players each season – ***The small details matter big.*** Their goal is to have as few surprises as possible come competition Day.

Champions have developed the habit of preparing well and taking care of small details. They understand that excellence is not achieved in a moment; it results from hundreds of small acts of preparation along the way.

Excellence is in the details.
Pay attention to every element and
excellence will come.

HABIT 42

THE HABIT OF GRATITUDE

"The real gift of gratitude is that the more grateful you are, the more present you become."

– Robert Holden

Ralph Waldo Emerson once said that, to achieve contentment, one should *"Cultivate the habit of being grateful for every good thing that comes to you, and to give thanks continually."*

It's always easy to tell the nature of an individual or group of people. People of high character and values display appreciation, humility, and gratefulness. There is nothing more impressive than, after a game, seeing athletes, coaches, or teams seek the officials, volunteers, and anyone else who has contributed to simply thank them. They recognize all who contribute tirelessly behind the scenes to make their day a little bit better. These kinds of behaviors display a high level of respect, humility, and appreciation.

Gratitude is an action, not just a thought or feeling. Don't presume others know that you appreciate them. It requires being more mindful, and we discover in grateful people that they recognize the small things that can so easily go unnoticed.

It reminds me of a piece I once read in Brad Gilbert's book, *"I've Got Your Back"*. Gilbert, a former world top four Tennis player himself, who coached Andre Agassi, was working with the American number one player, Andy Roddick. One of the first lessons Gilbert passed onto a young Andy was on displaying more gratitude and respect. After each tournament, win or lose, Gilbert would remind Andy to personally thank all the officials, transportation crew, ball kids, etc. before leaving the site. Admittingly easier to do when you win, but he did it. Andy would go on to become a hall of famer and one of the most likable personalities in the game.

Here are a few things you can be grateful for:

- Coaches
- Parents
- Teammates
- Event organizers
- Fans and Supporters
- Support staff
- Cleaning Crew
- Officials and Volunteers
- Your health
- Transportation

Besides sports, gratitude and appreciation have been shown to increase our happiness and our physical and mental health. It's been proven in worldwide studies that teams and organizations who display gratitude often have better relationships, a feeling of togetherness, and produce better results.

What about you? Do you show appreciation and thank others? After your next practice, team event, or match, make it an effort to express your gratitude and thanks to others in attendance. Showing gratitude is one of the simplest yet most powerful things we can do for each other. A simple *"thanks"* or a note of appreciation goes a long way. Champion athletes have developed the habit of practicing gratitude.

Someone helped you at practice today?
Someone drove you to the game?
Someone helped you with your homework?
Someone encouraged and supported you today?
Someone prepared you a meal today?
Someone gave you feedback on how to improve?

...then thank them and say you appreciate them.

Gratitude is an action, not just a thought or feeling. Don't presume others know that you appreciate them – tell them!

HABIT 43

THE HABIT OF EMBRACING THE MESSINESS

"Failure happens all the time. It happens every day in practice. What makes you better is how you react to it."

– Mia Hamm

Success is never a coincidence. Anything worth accomplishing never comes easy. If it was easy, everyone would do it. Achieving anything of meaning and significance involves some level of self-questioning, doubt, and discomfort along the way. Ask any Champion and they will tell you that success didn't come without them failing multiple times.

One of the most famous quotes about failure comes from the great NBA Basketball player, Michael Jordan. He said: *"I have missed over 9,000 shots in my career. I've lost almost 300 games. 26 times, I've been trusted to take the game winning shot and missed. I've failed over and over and over in my life. And that is why I succeed."*

Succeeding and mastering any craft never comes easy and making progress never looks like a straight line that points upwards. At times, the resemblance is more like a bowl of spaghetti!

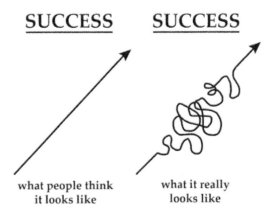

what people think   what it really
it looks like   looks like

To succeed in sports and in life, it's important that you learn how to handle setbacks, disappointments, and failures. Like Michael Jordan implies in the above-mentioned quote, failure is the tuition you pay for success. However, what is crucial to highlight here is that it's during these difficult and challenging times where the most progress is made.

Sometimes you can work your socks off and not see immediate results. It's normal to think that, just because you are putting in the hard work, everything should fall into place and happen for you. Unfortunately, life doesn't always work that way. During difficult and challenging times, the most important thing is to keep putting in the work and believe in it, because you never know how close you are to making that breakthrough. When you keep believing and trusting in yourself, the results will come. As Tennis star, Venus Williams, once said, *"You have to believe in yourself when no one else does, that's what makes you a winner right there."* It's during these challenging times that mental toughness, resilience, and grit are developed.

The frustration you feel when you aren't making fast enough progress will test you. At times, there will be voices in your head telling you it isn't possible, you aren't good enough, and maybe you should quit.

Remember:

- Challenges and obstacles are inevitable and necessary on the path to success

- Failure is not the opposite of success - it's a part of it

- The only failure in life is quitting. You're supposed to fail sometimes. It's a core part of the human experience. What matters is how you respond to it

Next time you feel you aren't making any progress, try to remind yourself about the bowl of spaghetti. Like the Champions do, see the frustration and messiness as a part of the process, and remember that nothing worth achieving in life ever comes easily.

Your biggest competition will always be yourself. Don't worry about what everyone else is doing. Just focus on becoming the best version of yourself.

HABIT 44

THE HABIT OF BREATHING

"Using certain breathing techniques has helped me become more present. It helps me remember that this moment, is the most important one."

– Kelly Slater

Sports are littered full of stories of athletes and teams choking emotionally and mentally under pressure. Maybe you've even experienced this unpleasant feeling, and I'm sure you will agree it's one of the most distressing and helpless feelings there is.

Working closely with athletes over the years has revealed that the *fear of failure* is one of the biggest reasons athletes choke or break down under pressure. It occurs when they are too focused and/or worried about the outcome instead of being engaged in the present moment.

Choking is something that every high-level performing athlete has experienced in their career. In sports, choking usually happens when you are in control but then suddenly, you feel overcome by the stress and pressure of it all. This causes you to overthink things and panic. From this, your mind and body prevent you from functioning and performing at your 'norm'.

To overcome this, one of the most useful and successful techniques centers on the concept of focused and applied breathing. This is a technique Champion athletes such as two-time Tennis Grand Slam Champion, Mary Pierce, would incorporate into her match routine between points. As a fierce competitor who kept a great composure on the court, it helped Mary remain calm and in control of her thoughts and emotions.

Another great example of a World-class athlete who used breathing to better his performance is NHL Hockey player, Glen Hanlon. The Canadian who played for the New York Rangers and Vancouver Canucks, said, *"What helped me was when I worked on my breathing, specifically, using my breathing to stay sharp and focused under pressure."*

When we use proper breathing techniques in sports, it helps:

- Decrease our stress and muscle tension
- Sharpen our focus
- Calm our nerves
- Minimize negative thoughts
- Regain our focus and composure

For breathing, Champions see it as a mental advantage that helps them stay composed and in control. The engine determines the level of performance their muscles will deliver. Unfortunately, proper breathing is often an overlooked component by many athletes.

A few years ago, I worked with a professional female Golfer from Korea who struggled with anxiety and nerves. In the bigger competitions such as the majors, she admittingly experienced choking a few times, especially when playing in front of large audiences or televised events. Before teeing off or making a crucial putt, she described the feeling as someone squeezing her tightly around her chest, making it difficult for her to breathe. She would have no feeling in her hands, which was problematic when holding a club or putter. However, after we introduced breathing techniques into her pre-shot rituals, she eventually overcame her demons. It was a process that took around six months of practice to improve.

As an athlete, working on your breathing should become an essential part of your training program. Maybe it's something to consider including in your routine or rituals, especially if you sometimes experience anxiety or nerves when competing. How you breathe has much to do with your athletic performance and your quality of life. Like the Champions, develop the habit of focusing on your breathing more.

*90% of the time, it's your mind,
not your body, that limits you.
With a Champion's mindset,
you can overcome almost any obstacle.*

HABIT 45

THE HABIT OF COMPETING HARD WHEN THE CHIPS ARE DOWN

"The hard days are the best because that's when Champions are made, so if you push through, you can push through anything."

– Gabby Douglas

As an athlete, every time you step out to compete, you are hoping that you will perform to your expectations. But, that's not always possible. Not even the best athletes in the world get to perform or compete the way they would like. The truth is that, no matter how well you prepare, it doesn't always guarantee you'll win. But it certainly gives you the best chance.

There's a great quote by Deena Kaster, the former American Marathon record holder and Olympic medalist. She said, *"As athletes, we have ups and downs. Unfortu-*

nately, you can't always pick the days they come on." It's a great quote because, come competition time, things aren't always going to go the way you had wished. However, the main difference in the outcome depends on how you approach it. Champions always try their hardest and give their best, regardless of the situation.

The great athletes don't fall to pieces or quit when things aren't going to plan or how they envisioned they would. They don't make excuses or place blame. They embrace the pressure and keep competing hard with a winning attitude and mindset. The most important thing for them to know is that, when it's game, set, and match, they are at peace knowing they gave it their absolute all.

I once asked a former Olympic Table Tennis player from China how many times she felt she played the 'perfect match' during her professional playing career. After giving it some thought, she replied, *"Probably no more than three or four times over 14 years on the tour."* She explained that, as a player, it's impossible to play your perfect game every time you step out to compete and, when she had learned to accept this, it helped her become a much better player.

One of the fastest growing sports in the United States is Pickleball. One of the most dominant male players in the game is Ben Johns. His sister, Hannah Johns, a commentator for the sport, mentioned that one reason why Ben has been so dominant over the years, was his ability to *outmaneuver* his opponents even when he wasn't playing well. In Hannah's words, *"Even when Ben is not at his best, he will still out strategize you. He's thinking 6 or 7 shots ahead."*

Athletes: Accepting you won't always play the perfect match or perform the way you'd like to every time you compete is paramount to your success. Sometimes you will just have to grind hard and *win ugly*. Remember, you can't always win on your terms and that you give yourself the best chance of success when you maintain a positive energy and keep competing hard.

Champions succeed because:

- They stay accountable for their own journey

- They accept they won't always have their 'A' game

- They stay positive under pressure

- They don't make excuses or blame others

- They compete until the end

Champions know that the biggest asset in life is a positive mindset. They have developed the habit of competing hard and believing in themselves, especially when the chips are down. **A negative mindset will never produce positive results.** As Alex Morgan, a World Cup winner and longtime member of the United States Women's Soccer team said, *"Always work hard, never give up, and fight until the end because it's never really over until the whistle blows."*

How resilient and mentally tough are you when the chips are down?

Being mentally tough is when you choose to keep a positive attitude when things aren't going your way.

HABIT 46

THE HABIT OF AIMING FOR PROGRESS, NOT PERFECTION

"Perfectionism is not self-improvement. Perfectionism is, at its core, about trying to earn approval and acceptance."

– Brene Brown

There's a great advertisement from clothing giant, Nike, that features Grand Slam Tennis Champion, Emma Raducanu. It begins with her saying, *"I was such a little perfectionist. I would go crazy if I didn't hit the balls in the right place. But I've definitely grown, and I've learned that perfectionism isn't a destination."* What Emma is alluding to here is common in competitive junior athletes growing up.

Perfectionism can be both an asset and a liability to the athlete. One advantage is that it can drive you to work harder and continually want to improve. However, perfectionism can also be one reason why some athletes don't progress beyond a certain level due to unrealistic expectations and a self-critical nature. Because of this, they often sabotage their own performances and more important, diminish the enjoyment of what they are doing. Often, perfectionists are never satisfied with the work they've done. It always reminds me of the famous Russian author, Leo Tolstoy who once said, *"If you look for perfection, you'll never be content."*

Perfectionists place a lot of expectations on their own shoulders and feel like a failure if they don't live up to them. They are also afraid to make mistakes and fail, especially when competing. When I asked Sarah Hirini, an Olympic medalist and captain of the New Zealand women's Sevens Rugby team about this, she agreed that perfectionism can be a barrier to becoming a great athlete and competitor. In Sarah's words, *"The great players aren't afraid to make mistakes or bring out their skills when needed, especially in tight games. They play with freedom, and it always looks like they are enjoying themselves. This is what makes them even more dangerous."* Listening to Sarah's answer, the one word that really jumped out for me was *'freedom.'* When you play with freedom you aren't being held captive by perfectionism, outcomes, or the fear of failure.

Examples of why perfectionism can hold you back:

- It can add extra pressure
- You have the feeling you will never be good enough
- It can set unrealistic expectations
- It can steal the fun and enjoyment out of doing what you love

For the perfectionist, it's natural to focus on what's <u>not</u> going well. This kind of mindset eventually depletes you of your self-belief and confidence because you are always doubting yourself and your preparation. Think about that for a second; you put in all those hours of hard work only to come to competition time and self-sabotage through an unhealthy quest for perfectionism.

Champions who chase excellence instead of perfection:

- Build confidence through self-reflecting on the positives

- Focus on the process instead of the outcome

- Have a greater trust in their skills instead of trying too hard

- Replace expectations with more manageable goals

Aim for excellence, not perfection. Break your perfectionism before it breaks you. Don't allow an *'A+ or nothing'* mentality become your greatest opponent. Remember that a B+ performance is sometimes good enough to be the victor. Focus on giving your best effort and be happy with that.

*"You're never chasing perfection.
You're learning how
to form great habits."*

– Swin Cash

HABIT 47

THE HABIT OF STAYING OPEN-MINDED

"A mind is like a parachute.
It doesn't work if it is not open."

– Frank Zappa

The Irish playwright, George Bernard Shaw, once said, "*Progress is impossible without change, and those who cannot change their minds cannot change anything*". Many years later, that quote still rings true. I've seen it with my own eyes. People who are more open-minded make more progress and get further ahead in life.

The ability to keep an open mind is one of the greatest assets you can have. It means considering lots of different possibilities and not just sticking to one belief. With your game, what worked last season might not necessarily work for you now. At certain stages in an athlete's career, they will have to make difficult and uncomfortable choices. When you are open-minded, you approach challenges differently. You are more focused on learning than on the outcomes.

For the athlete, staying open-minded can be a powerful and positive trait. It not only allows you to see things differently, but it also empowers you to think critically and rationally. When you are open-minded, you are not afraid to try new things and welcome feedback. It's something Jesse Kriel, a member of the South African Rugby team and a World Cup winner pointed out to me when I asked him what it meant to be a coachable player. He said, *"Being coachable is about having an open mind and being open to new ideas. It's about accepting feedback, regardless of how experienced you are or how much you've achieved in the game. To keep improving you need to keep challenging your skillset, you need to be brave and not be afraid to fail."*

If you say you are in the pursuit of excellence but are not open to other ideas, opinions, and perspectives, it will always be difficult for you to improve and further your development. It's difficult to keep growing when you continually surround yourself with the same old ideas and beliefs. Don't be afraid to challenge your beliefs, as progress requires unlearning. Becoming the best version of yourself requires you to continuously revisit your beliefs.

Many well-known athletes have sought different coaches and mentors to help advise and guide them throughout their careers. This enables them to keep learning and evolving. It's admirable to be loyal to the people who have helped you, but it's not always beneficial to continually hear the same voices. Being open-minded to different ideas and perspectives can help, while being stuck in your old ways and beliefs can limit your growth and progress.

Champion performers and open-minded people are:

- Curious to hear what their coaches and support team think

- Able to have their ideas or beliefs challenged

- Always looking for ways to improve

- Able to receive feedback better

- Receptive and don't get angry or defensive

Each day becomes a unique opportunity to nurture the habits supporting our growth while letting go of the behaviors and mindsets that are keeping us from achieving our greatest potential. Having convictions can be great, but strong or set beliefs does not negate an open mind. Pushing your boundaries and learning new things energizes and inspires you.

*Don't fall in love with success.
Fall in love with
the habits that bring success.*

HABIT 48

HABIT OF MENTAL HEALTH AWARENESS

"Mental health isn't just an athlete thing. What you do for a living doesn't have to define who you are. This is an everyone thing."

– Kevin Love

When watching a Champion athlete perform on television or live, we can easily think that they are almost superhuman. Being in awe of their incredible skills and abilities, we can sometimes place them on a pedestal. However, regardless of what people may think, these individuals are no different to you and me. They also have their everyday challenges, struggles and obstacles to overcome.

In an interview on World Mental Health Day, Formula 1 race car driver, Charles Leclerc said, *"Growing up, I remember watching all the Formula One drivers on TV and thinking they probably didn't have any difficult days. They always looked so confident and strong, but* now being in this position, there are some days worse than others."

With both internal and external pressures to perform in a sport, it can be challenging for a person's mental health. I speak from experience, as I too, had my fair share of struggles as a former professional athlete. Looking back, my biggest mistake was keeping things to myself and not seeking help.

According to a study done at the University of Michigan - School of Public Health, it's believed that over 33% of all college students experience significant symptoms of depression or other mental health issues.

Social Media:

One area that plays a big part these days with our mental health is the use of social media. Popular platforms such as Tik-Tok, Twitter, and Instagram have granted us unfiltered access to athletes at all hours of the day. This places athletes under the spotlight and opens them up for criticism, which impacts how they see themselves when they're playing their sport. **Your mental health will always matter more than any result.**

While chatting with a college coach one afternoon on this topic, she informed me that one of the biggest mistakes student-athletes make after a game is intentionally scrolling through their own social media accounts looking for any likes, comments, or mentions. She believes this might be one of the main reasons many athletes suffer from mental health problems such as depression, loss of confidence, and self-image issues.

Never forget that your energy and mental well-being are two of your most precious commodities. Protect them with everything you've got and know that not everyone deserves access to these. If you want to protect your mental health and well-being, refrain from engaging or arguing with strangers online. It's wasted energy and time. Conversing with trollers and people who don't have your best interests at heart is much the same as fighting with a pig in mud. George Bernard Shaw said it best, *"I learned long ago, never to wrestle with a pig. You get dirty, and besides, the pig likes it."*

Identity:

With your identity, realize that who you are isn't defined by what you've done as an athlete. Your results or accomplishments don't define who you are. You may think winning that medal or achieving your dream goal will *make your life.* I promise you, it won't. I know this to be true after being with many gold medal winning Olympians and world-class athletes. The majority will tell you 'that feeling' wears off quickly. Never get too high on the highs and never get too low on the lows. Keep a healthy perspective.

Question: If your athletic career was to suddenly end tomorrow, would you be prepared for the next chapter? Don't wait until the end of your career to think, *'what's next?'* The reality is that, as athletes, we don't always get to choose our last match, race, or retirement date. It sometimes chooses us. While you are still competing, lay down the foundations for the next chapter of your life.

When it comes to your identity, your relationship with yourself and the relationships you build with others will define your life. Aim to build your identity around who you are as a person, not around what you do or have accomplished.

Your self-worth isn't determined by what you've achieved.
When you stop basing your identity and value on these things, your happiness and mental health improves.

HABIT 49

THE HABIT OF BELIEVING IN YOUR DREAMS

"The only limit to the height of your achievements is the reach of your dreams and the willingness to work hard for them."

– Michelle Obama

Sometimes, it's so easy to forget that all the great Champions were once humble beginners. The thought of playing a sport at a high level seemed so far away, but ask any Champion and they will tell you they once had a dream and vision of being a Champion one day. In fact, there is an excellent video of a young Novak Djokovic being interviewed at the age of 7. When asked what his goal in Tennis was, he said, *"To be the number one player in the world."*

In my job, I often come across athletes who have either lost belief or sight of their dreams and aspirations.

The interesting thing I've found is that many don't realize just how close they are to breaking through.

Champions have all had their 'naysayers and doubters'; people that told them they weren't good enough and wouldn't make it. In fact, you'd be surprised how many great athletes and performers were cut from teams or told they wouldn't amount to much. Some of those include:

- NBA player, Carmelo Anthony, was cut from his High School basketball team for being "too short". He became a star player for the New York Knicks and Team USA

- Ballet dancer, Misty Copeland, danced at age 13, and was told she was too old to make it as an elite dancer. She was informed that she'd never make it to a major company due to her muscular frame. Misty became the American Ballet Theater's first African American female principal dancer

- Lionel Messi, was told he'd never make it to the professional ranks due to being "too small". Lionel won the *World's Best Football Player Award* a record seven times

- Tom Brady was told in college he lacked the athleticism and ability to play at the highest level. Tom became arguably the greatest quarterback to ever play in the NFL

If someone doubts your abilities, use it as positive motivation to improve. If you get dropped from the team, don't blame, whine, or complain. Instead, use it as fuel to win your place back. That's what a Champion would do. Champions don't get bitter, they get better. A great example is the Ice Hockey player, Zdeno Chara, who became one of the game's best defensemen. Zdeno was never supposed to make it past the junior ranks as several teams cut him. After playing in the NHL for 24 seasons, he said, *"My message to all the kids who have been cut – it's amazing what you can accomplish by putting your mind to it and working hard."* Also, remember that being under-estimated is one of the biggest competitive advantages you can have.

Many athletes fail to ever realize their potential because of self-imposed beliefs about their abilities and how far they can go. The message is simple: Always believe in your dreams and in yourself. If you can't see yourself as a Champion, then the chances of you being one will be slim. **Remember that winners are not people who never fail, but people who never quit.** When French Formula 1 race car driver Pierre Gasly was asked in an interview about his journey to the top, he said, *"I'd always tell myself to believe in my dreams and believe in myself. I met a lot of people who tried to crush my dreams and that's sad. If you really want something, you can do it. I've always had that mentality."*

When I asked Laura Wilkinson, an Olympic gold medalist in Diving, what she had seen in the athletes who made it to an elite level, she said, *"What separates those who reach the top is their undying commitment to the belief that their goals and dreams, however crazy they may be, are attainable and they are willing to do whatever it takes every single day to make it a reality."*

There will be doubters. There will be obstacles. There will be mistakes. But, by developing the habit of discipline, hard work, and having a rock-solid belief in yourself, you can achieve your goals and dreams.

Always believe in yourself.
Never let the opinion of another get in
the way of who you can become.
Know that greatness is in you.

HABIT 50

THE HABIT OF ENJOYING THE JOURNEY

*"Enjoy the journey, enjoy every moment, and
quit worrying about winning and losing."*

– Matt Biondi

Whilst writing my second book, *'Champion Minded: Achieving Excellence in Sports & Life'*, I got to interview around 150 former professional and collegiate level athletes. One of the questions I posed to each was: *"When you look back on your playing days, what is one of the biggest regrets you hold to this day?"* Almost every athlete answered that they wished they had enjoyed the moments along the journey more.

The journey refers to the things we can so easily overlook or take for granted. It's about the everyday happenings such as the team practices, the matches, the travels, the meals together as a team, sharing hotel rooms, the wins and losses, the injuries, your teammates, your competitors, coaches, etc.

Covid-19 times taught us we can never take a day for granted. During the pandemic, there were way more important things to worry about than canceled sports events or closed gyms. However, it made us realize how much we missed spending time with our teammates or competing. It put things in perspective.

The next time you're thinking *"I have to train today",* try change that thinking to *"I get to train today."* Learn to appreciate every moment you get to play the sport you love. An athletic career can go by fast. Coming from a background in professional sports, I can attest those were some of the most enjoyable years of my life. As Simone Biles, the four-time Olympic gold medalist in Gymnastics says, *"If you're having fun, that's when the best memories are built."* Of course, I'm still lucky to partake in sports to this day, but looking back, the time spent with my fellow teammates and coaches is something I'll never take for granted.

When I asked Roland Schoeman, a world record holder and Olympic gold medalist in Swimming, if he had any regrets as an athlete, he said, *"Looking back, I wish I'd maybe enjoyed the journey a little more. Even when I was competing at all those Olympics Games, I would lock myself away in my room only to come out when I was going for practice or to compete. I wish I'd taken in the whole experience a little more, the Olympic Village, meeting other athletes and watching other events, etc."*

If you only wait to celebrate the wins and not the everyday processes in which it takes to win, you miss the whole point of what the journey is all about. Playing sports should be about challenging yourself and finding joy in the very act. The journey should always take precedence over the destination itself. I've learned that the ones who get the most out of the journey learn to find joy and fulfillment in the everyday process.

When reflecting on her career and journey as a professional athlete, Bronte Campbell, an Australian Olympic gold medalist in Swimming said, *"I didn't do it so much for racing, I did it for the moments between the races, the people I got to meet, the places I got to visit etc. It was about enjoying the journey and realizing that there is no destination."* Bronte reminds us that the greatest lessons are bestowed in the journey itself.

If you are still practicing and competing today, be grateful. Appreciate the moments; trust me, they don't last forever. Squeeze the juice out of every day. Don't waste an opportunity and don't leave any regrets on the table.

Along the journey, **instead of focusing on what you are getting, focus on the person you are becoming.** Ultimately, your habits will determine who you become. Your habits are the channel through which you develop your deepest beliefs about yourself.

Enjoy the moments.
The rides on the team bus.
The fun and banter with your
teammates. The team practices.
The meals you shared together.
One day, those moments won't be
around anymore.

Conclusion:

I am confident that if you apply the habits and information provided in this book, extraordinary things will happen.

No matter how far you progress as an athlete, the time and effort you have invested throughout all those years will never go to waste. The habits you have created and the lessons you will have gained from your athletic journey are all transferable skills in business and in life.

Remember that your coaches and parents can only do so much to help you improve. Ultimately, how far you go lies in your hands. **It's all on you.** I encourage you to take on these habits and build the consistency it requires to be a Champion.

I believe that you can achieve your dreams and goals, but to do so, you must first believe it's possible. Dare to be great and don't allow a limited mindset to hold you back from what you can become. You can do great things, but only if you are willing to do the work.

Be proud of yourself. Be proud of the fact that you are trying. Be proud of all the obstacles you've already overcome. We sometimes sell ourselves short when it comes to acknowledging the work that has gone into past accomplishments.

Finally, appreciate the people who love and support you. Most of all, learn to enjoy the moments, the journey and all that it brings.

Excellence is in you.
Allistair

Do it once = Action
Do it twice = Repetition
Do it a few times = Behavior
Do it consistently = Habit

Speaking & Consulting

Alongside his consulting services, Allistair is also an internationally acclaimed keynote speaker and has spoken in over 50 countries around the globe.

Some topics he speaks on include:
Leadership & Coaching
Team & Organizational Culture
Mindset & High Performance

For enquiries, please e-mail:
info@allistairmccaw.com

Social Media:

Twitter: @allistairmccaw
Instagram: @bechampionminded
Website: www.allistairmccaw.com
#ChampionHabits

I'D LOVE TO HEAR YOUR FEEDBACK!

Thank you so much for reading my book and I hope you enjoyed it. I would be most grateful if you could take a few minutes of your time to leave a rating and review on *Amazon*.

Your feedback means the world to me!

Special Thanks...

Finally, this book wouldn't have been possible without the editing of Michelle Eyles (ME your VA) and the cover design and layout of Eli 'The Book Guy' Blyden.

OTHER WORKS BY ALLISTAIR MCCAW

Printed in Great Britain
by Amazon

56141436R30185